AGILE FOUNDATIONS

BCS, THE CHARTERED INSTITUTE FOR IT

BCS, The Chartered Institute for IT champions the global IT profession and the interests of individuals engaged in that profession for the benefit of all. We promote wider social and economic progress through the advancement of information technology, science and practice. We bring together industry, academics, practitioners and government to share knowledge, promote new thinking, inform the design of new curricula, shape public policy and inform the public.

Our vision is to be a world-class organisation for IT. Our 70,000 strong membership includes practitioners, businesses, academics and students in the UK and internationally. We deliver a range of professional development tools for practitioners and employees. A leading IT qualification body, we offer a range of widely recognised qualifications.

Further Information
BCS, The Chartered Institute for IT,
First Floor, Block D,
North Star House, North Star Avenue,
Swindon, SN2 1FA, United Kingdom.
T +44 (0) 1793 417 424
F +44 (0) 1793 417 444
www.bcs.org/contact

http://shop.bcs.org/

AGILE FOUNDATIONS
Principles, practices and frameworks

Peter Measey and Radtac

DSDM®, Atern® and AgilePM® are registered trademarks of Dynamic Systems Development Method Limited in the United Kingdom and other countries. Diagrams are copyright DSDM Consortium reproduced with permission.

Published by BCS Learning & Development Ltd, a wholly owned subsidiary of BCS, The Chartered Institute for IT, First Floor, Block D, North Star House, North Star Avenue, Swindon, SN2 1FA, UK.
www.bcs.org

ISBN: 978-1-78017-254-5
PDF ISBN: 978-1-78017-255-2
ePUB ISBN: 978-1-78017-256-9
Kindle ISBN: 978-1-78017-257-6

Ebook available

British Cataloguing in Publication Data.
A CIP catalogue record for this book is available at the British Library.

BCS books are available at special quantity discounts to use as premiums and sale promotions, or for use in corporate training programmes. Please visit our Contact us page at www.bcs.org/contact

Typeset by Lapiz Digital Services, Chennai, India.
Printed by Hobbs the Printers Ltd, Totton, Hampshire SO40 3WX

CONTENTS

LIST OF FIGURES AND TABLES

CONTRIBUTORS

Peter Measey (editor and main author) has over 30 years' experience in the computing sector, and has specialised in Agile since 1994. He has managed and contributed to many successful Agile transformations in the public and private sectors in the UK and internationally. Peter is CEO of Radtac Ltd, an Agile specialist consultancy and training organisation; a certified ScrumMaster, practitioner and trainer; a PMI–Agile certified practitioner; committee member of the BCS Agile Specialist Group; a certified DSDM trainer; a certified APMG Agile project management trainer; a certified PRINCE2 practitioner and ex-director of the DSDM Consortium. Peter has written all sections and chapters of the book not specifically mentioned as written by other authors below, and Peter has edited all sections.

Alex Gray is a Lean and Agile coach for Radtac Ltd. He has 18 years' experience in various IT roles and IT projects that cover software development, COTS product implementation, and infrastructure installation and upgrades. Alex is a certified ScrumMaster, Kanban practitioner, certified DSDM Atern Agile project management practitioner, certified collaboration architect, SAFe Agilist and a PRINCE2 practitioner. He is a certified trainer of APMG Agile project management, and BCS Foundation in Agile Practices. Alex is a member of the BCS Agile Panel and is co-author of the BCS Foundation in Agile Practices syllabus, examination, and course materials. Alex wrote sections 1.1 History of Agile (with Peter Measey); 1.2.2 12 Principles (with Peter Measey); 2.6 Empirical and defined processes (with Peter Measey); 6.3 The Agile lead (with Peter Measey); 8.1 Short feedback loops; 8.3 Daily stand-ups; 8.4 Show and tells; 8.6 Emergent documentation; 8.7 visual boards (with Peter Measey); 8.9 Focus on quality; 10.2 Deliver working software frequently; and 14.3 Dynamic systems development method (with Barbara Roberts).

Chris Berridge has spent the better part of 20 years in diverse industries in diverse countries experimenting with what makes the software development process effective – initially as a developer, then as a manager and, more recently, as a coach. He's fascinated by how often what he thought he knew turns out to be false in the light of new experience. In his current role, Chris leads large-scale Agile transformations. Chris was Agile Programme/Project Manager of the Year (UK Agile Awards 2011) and is a scaled Agile programme consultant, a certified ScrumMaster and a BCS certified Agile practitioner. Chris wrote sections 2.1 The Agile mindset; 9.1 Motivated and talented individuals; 9.2 Emergent design from self-organising teams; 14.2 Scrum; 14.5 Kanban; 14.6 Lean software development; 14.7 Lean start-up; and 14.8 Scaled Agile framework (with Darren Wilmshurst).

Darren Wilmshurst has spent almost 30 years in the corporate environment holding senior positions first within retail banking and then in travel and logistics. Darren joined Radtac Ltd in 2012, having contributed a number of business transformations in the private sector. Darren is the Finance Director and Head of Consultancy of Radtac Ltd. Darren is a chartered professional of two industries: an associate of the Chartered Institute of Bankers as well as a Chartered IT Professional. He's also a PRINCE2 practitioner, certified ScrumMaster, accredited Kanban practitioner, DSDM Atern Agile PM practitioner, APMG facilitation practitioner and a SAFe program consultant. Darren is the founder of the Kent Scrum User Group, the treasurer of the BCS Kent Branch and board member of the ASA South East Regional Management Board. Darren wrote sections 6.1 The customer; 6.4 The stakeholders; 8.8 Sustainable pace; and 14.8 Scaled Agile framework (SAFe) (with Chris Berridge).

Richard Levy is a software developer and Agile coach for Radtac Ltd. With 20 years in the IT industry, Richard has developed software in multiple languages and industries, from safety-critical flight control to e-commerce and travel industry web platforms. Most recently, Richard has moved into lightweight web application and mobile development. Richard is a certified Java developer, ScrumMaster and developer, Kanban practitioner and SAFe Agilist, as well as a certified trainer of the Certified Scrum Developer course. Richard wrote Section 14.1 eXtreme Programming.

Michael Short has spent the majority of his career directing businesses in the pharmaceutical and biotech sector in Europe and the USA in various senior positions (e.g. CEO, President, Vice President of Business Development, Country Head). Michael is COO and Head of Culture at Radtac and received his MBA from Aston in 1992. Michael has used Agile approaches and frameworks alongside organisational development understanding to drive value creation for investors and clients. He is a CSM and Scaled Agilist. Michael's focus has been to provide clarity for businesses on their people and bring Agile approaches to non-IT environments. He is proud that Radtac believes fundamentally in the innate ability of people to drive an organisation's evolution. Michael wrote Section 9.3.2 Lencioni – the five dysfunctions of teams.

Barbara Roberts is a DSDM and Agile coach, focusing mainly on Agile transformations in large corporate organisations. Barbara is DSDM-certified as an advanced practitioner, trainer, coach, examiner and consultant, as well as being a certified facilitator, certified Agile leader, advanced practitioner and a certified Scrum practitioner. She has been a member of the DSDM Board for many years, previously responsible for professional development and more recently for DSDM product innovation. Barbara ran one of the six DSDM early-adopter projects in 1995 and has been heavily involved in DSDM and all things Agile ever since. Barbara also led the creation and launch of DSDM's Agile Project Management (AgilePM®) and was initially the Chief Examiner for AgilePM for APMG. Barbara wrote the following sections: 14.3 DSDM (with Alex Gray); 14.4 Agile project management; and reviewed the whole book.

Les Oliver (chief proofreader). Les has worked in IT for over 40 years. He was introduced to Agile in the spring of 2000 and sold his first Agile project in the Easter of that year. He has worked with global IT suppliers and specialist SMEs, where his clients have included international banks, global brands, high street retailers, start-ups and SMEs, central and local government and public sector organisations. Les is an ex-director of the DSDM Consortium and has presented at several Agile seminars and conferences.

Lazaro Wolf is a Lean transformation consultant committed to help organisations on their journey towards Agility. As a passionate advocate of Lean thinking, systemic leadership and collaboration, Lazaro delivered global mission-critical projects for SaaS companies, the Big Four and the European Commission in the last 10 years. Despite starting his career in user experience and visual arts, he was quickly lured into the world of change management and process improvement. He achieved professional recognitions – such as Fellow of BCS (FBCS), Member of the Chartered Management Institute (MCMI) and Certified Scrum Professional (CSP) – and provides consulting and training in Lean Kanban (LKU Accredited Kanban Trainer) and Agile thinking (BCS Agile Foundation Trainer). Lazaro is the secretary of the BCS Agile Methods Specialist Group, organising events for the Agile community, such as the London Lean Kanban Day (LLKD). Frequently, he rumbles on Twitter at @lazarowolf and on his personal blog. When not researching or with an Agile team, Lazaro can be found in the kitchen, usually setting the smoke alarm off with his experimentations on molecular cooking. He wrote sections 8.2 Face-to-face communication; 8.5 Retrospectives (with Peter Measey); 11.1 Business people and developers must work together; and 12.1 Embrace change.

SECTION REVIEWERS

The section reviewers have generally reviewed one or a few sections of this book, so we have highlighted their name on the section they reviewed only; they have not reviewed the whole book.

Randal Cooper (Radtac) – technically reviewed numerous sections

Jose Casal-Jimenez (BCS Agile Methods Specialist Group Committee Chair) – reviewed a few sections

Matt Roadnight reviewed Section 14.2 Scrum

Barbara Roberts reviewed Section 14.3 DSDM®

David J Anderson reviewed Section 14.5 Kanban

Tom Poppendieck reviewed Section 14.6 Lean software development

Dean Leffingwell reviewed Section 14.8 Scaled Agile framework

GLOSSARY

Agile Operating Model The holistic and simple definition of what an organisation, programme, project or team mean when they use the term 'Agile'. This could be a single Agile framework or an integrated implementation of many frameworks, the latter being much more likely. Agile operating models align to the 'Agile Manifesto'.

Agile Persona Someone (a person or group) who will interact with the system being built, also known as a 'user'.

Backlog An ordered list of requirements/stories that the customer wants.

Baseline Plan The plan that defines the start point from which an evolving product starts, normally high level.

Best Practice The learned best approach for something at a particular point in time, best practice evolves over time.

Business The customers (see Section 6.1), stakeholders (see Section 6.4) and users of the product.

Command and Control A style of management where the manager commands the team to do something and then controls them to do it. This style of management is the opposite of Agile self-organising teams.

Commitment Plan Typically a detailed forecast for a short period of time, also known as iteration/sprint (or time-box) plans.

Cost of Delay The cost of delaying an investment decision.

Customer The person/people who own the product (e.g. known as a 'Product Owners' or 'Business Ambassadors' in certain frameworks).

Definition of Done Normally a list that defines the complete product that must be delivered; must be standard across the team (see Section 10.2).

Definition of Ready Normally a list that defines when artefacts within the delivery process are ready (e.g. story ready to go into iteration/sprint).

DevOps Viewing the development and operation of a software system as one continuous delivery value chain.

Environment The combination of all factors within an organisation, project, team etc. that drives suitability of a delivery or governance framework. In a dynamic environment, where things change all the time, an Agile framework would be suitable.

Facilitated Workshops Groups of people coming together in a forum to achieve a stated objective, the achievement of which is facilitated by a workshop facilitator. Many activities (such as planning) within Agile are delivered within facilitated workshops.

Feature A feature of the system that the customer wants, normally described as a story and ordered within a backlog.

Iteration/Sprint A short focused amount of delivery effort to deliver stories within an iteration/sprint goal, normally between 2 and 4 weeks.

Iteration/Sprint Goal The goal that the team commit to in relation to an iteration/sprint plan.

Iteration/Sprint Plan The forecast of what will be delivered within a short focused 'sprint' by the team.

Knowledge Based Work Work where the main capital is knowledge, such as doctors, engineers and information technology workers.

Noise Anything that interrupts the team within an iteration/sprint, noise causes significant disturbance within a team and causes lack of focus on delivery.

Regression Testing Primarily aimed at making sure that the software system operates in the same way it did before a change was made.

Requirements Described as 'stories' within most Agile frameworks (see Section 7.1).

Source Control System Part of software configuration management, manages the central repository of code versions, etc.

Stakeholder Any person or group who can help the team, or hinder.

Story A requirement or feature that may be delivered at some point; a story is a token to remind everyone that something may need to be delivered. Stories reside on the backlog.

Time-box A fixed period of time within which delivery is made, stories are prioritised within a time-box. With Agile projects, releases and iterations/sprints are all time-boxes.

User People who will use the product, known as 'Agile personas' within Agile.

Working Software Software that works, has all the elements associated with the 'Definition of Done' and is ready to deploy into an environment which should be the live production environment.

PREFACE

Why – This book has been written for two major reasons:

- It provides a foundation-level description of Agile from a generic perspective, not biased to any specific Agile framework. This means it will give you an excellent start point for your Agile journey that overviews all the key values, principles and practices of Agile, and then references out to further detail.
- As supporting material and a reference book for the BCS Agile Foundations syllabus, course and certification (bcs.org/agilecertified).

What – There are many Agile books available; however, the majority of them discuss specific Agile techniques or specific Agile frameworks. This book endeavours to give a rounded, unbiased view of Agile generically, not focusing on any one Agile framework's view. While Agile frameworks (see Chapter 14) have successfully been applied to business transformation projects, marketing, health service commissioning, and many other business sectors, this book mainly concentrates on Agile product delivery within the IT industry.

It contains many references to other excellent books, websites and people and acts as a single point from which to start your Agile journey. From the perception of the people involved in creating this book we are all still on the journey and long may we be so.

How – Many very experienced practitioners of Agile have been involved in authoring and reviewing this book. There are hundreds of years of shared practical experience that have been put into this book.

Agile is purposefully simple. For example, the Agile Manifesto itself consists of only 4 statements and 12 principles.

The majority of Agile frameworks are also purposefully simple. Indeed arguably the most used Agile framework as at 2015 is Scrum (see Section 14.2), which is one of the simplest Agile frameworks.

So how can something as simple as Agile require an 'Agile Foundations' book of around 55,000 words?

We have endeavoured to not only simply state what Agile is, with some guidance on how to do it; we have also focused heavily on why Agile should be used and what the fundamental thinking and science behind it is. Our strong belief is that a fundamental level of Agile understanding starts with an understanding of **why** Agile should be used and in what circumstances. As with many things, behind the simplicity there is complexity and we have represented what we think is an appropriate level of that complexity; however, our core guidance when implementing Agile is 'KISS': Keep It Simple.

The book is primarily designed so that the reader can reference particular areas of interest individually and that those areas stand on their own (e.g. Agile planning or stories). We have also provided many in-text references if the reader wishes to investigate a particular area further. However, we have also structured the book to flow end-to-end and therefore it also makes a great read from start to finish.

The book is structured into four major parts:

PART 1: 'Introducing Agile' (Chapters 1–4) outlines the major principles of Agile, the Agile mindset and other elements for a basic rounded understanding of Agile.

PART 2: 'A Generic Agile framework' (Chapters 5–8) goes through the major generic elements of most of the Agile frameworks and provides a solid grounding in the key elements of most Agile frameworks.

PART 3: 'Applying Agile principles' (Chapters 9–13) overviews thinking learned from the author's experience and from many other great reference sources; this part of the book is about why and how to apply Agile principles.

PART 4: 'Agile frameworks' introduces what we consider to be the major Agile frameworks. We have defined a 'major' framework as one that we see very regularly in our day-to-day work as Agile trainers and consultants.

Welcome fellow Agilista – You are about to embark on an extremely exciting journey that may well change your perceptions and even your whole career direction, as it has for many of us. We hope you get as much enjoyment reading this book as we have had creating it.

Peter Measey (peter.measey@radtac.co.uk) 2014

INTRODUCTION

From 11 to 13 February 2001, 17 software development gurus from different fields and method frameworks gathered at a retreat in Snowbird, Utah. All attendees were sympathetic to and driven by the need for an alternative to documentation-driven, heavyweight software development processes and the problems that these posed, such as late and over-budget delivery of less-than-satisfactory products.

From this meeting came the agreed 'Manifesto for Agile Software Development' (see Section 1.2), which is still the basis for the development and delivery of Agile frameworks and provides the single definition of 'Agile' that all these frameworks align to.

So what is Agile and what are its foundations?

- Agile is a collection of evolving delivery and management frameworks (see Chapter 14) for dynamic and innovative delivery environments – like IT deliveries.

- Individually and collectively the frameworks are focused on ensuring that the highest priority is to satisfy the customer through early and continuous delivery of valuable product.

To be flexible has become vital for a business in today's global markets and, therefore, the ability for IT systems and solutions to be equally flexible is essential. The purpose of Agile is to allow organisations to react to the increasingly dynamic opportunities and challenges of today's business world, in which IT has become one of the key enablers.

PART 1
INTRODUCING AGILE

1 WHAT IS AGILE?

1.1 THE HISTORY OF AGILE

'Standing on the shoulders of giants' is a particularly apt term when discussing the evolution of Agile, as Agile thinking is founded on the concepts and ideas behind many different IT governance and delivery frameworks. Table 1.1 shows the evolution of these frameworks (see Chapter 14) since the late 1940s, leading to what is now generically referred to as 'Agile'.

Table 1.1 History of Agile frameworks

Year	Development of framework
1948	Taiichi Ohno, Shigeo Shingo and Eiji Toyoda create the 'Toyota Way'. Many Agile concepts relate to Lean thinking
1985	Tom Gilb develops EVO (Gilb, n.d.)
1986	Barry Boehm works on Spiral (Boehm, 1986)
1990	Rapid Application Development (RAD) is documented (Martin J., n.d.)
1992	The Crystal family of methodologies is defined (Cockburn, 2004)
1994	Dynamic Systems Development Method is created (DSDM Consortium, 2014b)
1995	Ken Schwaber and Jeff Sutherland present a paper on Scrum at the OOPSLA (Object-Oriented Programming, Systems, Languages and Applications conference) (Sutherland, Patel, Casanave, Miller and Hollowell, 1995)
1996	Rational Unified Process (RUP) (IBMRational, n.d.)
1997	Feature Driven Development

(Continued)

Table 1.1 (Continued)

Year	Development of framework
1999	Kent Beck publishes *Extreme Programming (XP) Explained* (Beck, 2004)
2001	The Agile Manifesto is created (Agile Manifesto, 2001)
2003	Mary and Tom Poppendieck publish Lean Software Development (Poppendieck, 2003)
2007	David J. Anderson discusses Kanban at Agile 2007 (Anderson, 2010)
2009	Eric Ries speaks on Lean start-up (Ries, 2011)

Some Agile thinking is based on the 'Toyota Production System (TPS)' (Liker, 2004) or 'Lean', as it is now more widely known. For example, the concept of Visual Boards (see Section 8.7) is taken from TPS. However, as the name suggests, TPS is mainly related to manufacturing products on a production line. Agile thinking is more focused on Lean product development than it is on Lean manufacturing, because the dynamic environments in which Agile is implemented are more similar to a dynamic innovative Lean product environment than a Lean manufacturing environment where variability is specifically discouraged and repeatability encouraged. Innovation and creativity, two fundamentals of effective product development, are enabled by variability and disabled by focusing on repeatability.

Tom Gilb's 'Evo' and Barry Boehm's 'Spiral' approaches were incorporated into Agile thinking in the early 1990s into what became known as Rapid Application Development (RAD).

Many RAD frameworks up to this point had concentrated on product delivery with no great focus on project governance. The exception was DSDM (see Section 14.3), which was created in the mid-1990s and focused on delivery within projects.

In 1999, another key Agile framework was created called eXtreme Programming or 'XP' (see Section 14.1). While XP focuses more on the values and practices associated with the technical programming aspects of engineering software, many of the practices are now also being used effectively in generic product development.

An important point in the evolution of these frameworks occurred when the term 'RAD' became associated with delivery failure, and finally disappeared in the late 1990s. One of the reasons for this was that, in the late 1990s, many organisations were using the term RAD to describe their delivery method, whether it was actually RAD or not, because it had become the 'cool' name in town. This meant that teams and organisations pretended or imagined that they were doing RAD, but did it without actually changing any of their delivery and management culture and behaviours. This led to a lot of failed initiatives that were shaped in a traditional 'Waterfall' way (see Section 2.6.3) being described as 'failures of RAD' – even though they hadn't initially been properly set up as RAD projects. Fundamentally, a key point was misunderstood by many people: while RAD itself was easy, transforming to RAD could be extremely complex.

Also, the word 'Rapid' in 'Rapid Application Development' meant that the immediate and lasting impression was of speed rather than a balance of regular value delivery and quality, which proved inappropriate.

It was not until 2001, when the Agile Manifesto (see Section 1.2.1) was formulated, that a collective generic name and terms of reference that supported all the frameworks was defined, and Agile as a concept was born.

In the same year the first Scrum (see Section 14.2) book was authored by Ken Schwaber and Mike Beedle (Schwaber and Beedle, 2001). The book evolved the basic concepts of Scrum from a seminal paper in the 1986 *Harvard Business Review*, written by the godfathers of the Scrum Agile Process, Takeuchi and Nonaka (Takeuchi and Nonaka, 1986). Scrum has since grown into by far the most implemented Agile framework in the world.

Since that time, further evolution of Agile thinking has been achieved, and notable more recent frameworks include Lean software development (see Section 14.6) and Kanban (see Section 14.5), amongst others.

1.2 THE AGILE MANIFESTO

As mentioned in the Introduction, the Agile Manifesto provides the single definition of Agile and underlies the development and delivery of Agile frameworks. While its title 'The Manifesto for Agile Software Development' suggests that it is only applicable to software development, the values and principles described in the Manifesto can easily be applied to the development of many types of product.

The Manifesto describes 4 values and 12 supporting principles. The values set out in the Agile Manifesto are:

> We are uncovering better ways of developing software by doing it and helping others do it. Through this work we have come to value:
>
> Individuals and interactions *over* processes and tools.
>
> Working software *over* comprehensive documentation.
>
> Customer collaboration *over* contract negotiation.
>
> Responding to change *over* following a plan.
>
> That is, while there is value in the items on the right, we value the items on the left more.

Typically an Agile audit or health check will be performed against the 4 manifesto statements and the 12 manifesto principles. It may also be further refined by the key values and principles of whatever combination of Agile frameworks (see Chapter 14) is being implemented.

In this chapter, we will take a closer look at the manifesto's values and supporting principles.

1.2.1 Agile values

The four Agile Manifesto statements or values are described next and are further expanded in Chapters 9–12.

1.2.1.1 Individuals and interactions over processes and tools

While processes and tools provide significant value to software development teams and enable them to be Agile, the best processes and tools will not help them to deliver value to the customer without enabled and motivated people who interact effectively as a team (see Chapter 9).

1.2.1.2 Working software over comprehensive documentation

The vast majority of software products require supporting documentation; for example most software deliveries require technical user documentation (see Section 8.6) as without this documentation it will become extremely difficult to support and maintain the software product in the future and throughout its lifecycle. (See also Chapter 10.)

However, while fit-for-purpose documentation is key in an Agile delivery, the focus is on providing working software, and therefore adding value directly to the customer. This means that Agile demonstrates progress through regular visible incremental deliveries of a consistently working product (see Section 10.3). Each and every time a new increment of the product is delivered the customer can be assured that good, agreed progress is being made – and/or be aware in advance of any hindrances to progress. In Agile product development the documentation is kept as Lean as possible (see Section 8.6); only documentation that adds value to the stakeholders is produced and the production of the documentation is synchronised with the incremental delivery of the working product.

1.2.1.3 Customer collaboration over contract negotiation

In Agile it is important to create a consistently collaborative and open relationship between the customer and supplier (see Chapter 11 and Section 11.1), and to ensure that the customer and supplier acknowledge that an effective product cannot be developed without that collaboration. Obviously there are still contracts between customers and suppliers, however, contracts tend to focus on clarifying the collaboration and the working approach between the customer and supplier to ensure they can work together to a mutually satisfactory conclusion. This means that the Agile contract concentrates on enabling inspection and adaptation of the product, prioritisation and collaboration between all stakeholders.

This stands in contrast to a traditional 'Waterfall'-driven contract, in which the analysis and design stages will produce detailed documents that become fundamental parts of the contract (e.g. the requirement specification, functional specification etc.). The interaction between customer and supplier then becomes a negotiation based on the detailed documents that have been produced. This can create significant friction; for example, it may lead to each party trying to get the other to pay for changes to the contracted specifications. This can become a very significant problem where there is a large amount of change required to the contracted specifications.

1.2.1.4 Responding to change over following a plan

According to About.com, German military strategist Helmuth von Moltke wrote:

> 'No battle plan survives contact with the enemy.' As a result, he sought to maximise his chances of success by remaining flexible and ensuring that the transportation and logistical networks were in place to allow him to bring decisive force to the key points on the battlefield.
>
> (Hickman, 2014)

This principle is replicated in an Agile development: while there is a significant amount of focused planning (see Section 7.3; Chapter 12), this planning is designed to enable inspection and adaptation.

In essence the majority of Agile frameworks align to the following concepts:

- If programme/project plans are required, they are defined at a high level – these are baseline plans that are expected to change.
- If stage (or release) plans are required, they are defined at a mid level – again, these are baseline plans that are expected to change.
- Detailed work package or sprint/iteration plans (see Section 12.1) are commitment plans, the commitment being against an agreed goal (for example, an agreed increment of the product).

This means that up-front project plans and stage plans are not commitment plans; rather it is understood that these plans are forecast best guesses based on experience or factual evidence and change is anticipated as the project develops (see Section 7.3).

1.2.2 The Agile principles

There are 12 Agile principles that support the 4 manifesto statements.

1.2.2.1 Our highest priority is to satisfy the customer through early and continuous delivery of valuable software (see Section 10.1)

The entire focus of Agile is to deliver value to the customer as frequently, consistently and regularly as possible. By continuously delivering product increments that provide additional value, the customer is much more likely to be satisfied and involved. It also means that they are more likely to understand and buy into the product being delivered.

This means that in an Agile delivery, it is essential that product stories (the required features of the product – see Section 7.1) are expressed in a way that makes sense to everyone in the team, the technical people and business people. Generally the order of the stories to be delivered will be largely driven by business value; however, the team also need to ensure that the optimum way to deliver the product from a technical perspective is considered (amongst many other considerations).

1.2.2.2 Welcome changing requirements, even late in development. Agile processes harness change for the customer's competitive advantage (see Section 12.1)

In an Agile delivery, the team and customer endeavour to refine and break down complex business needs into stories (features or components of the product – see Section 7.1) that can be understood, defined, tested and delivered fast. This approach enables the entire team to inspect, learn and adapt as they iteratively deliver product features via stories.

As the team continuously delivers value-add stories to the customer, they can also harness and demonstrate change to the customer's competitive advantage. As they collaborate effectively and reciprocally with the customer, they can identify and learn/evolve more effective ways to deliver added value (see Section 10.1).

Agile also significantly reduces the risk of the team spending a significant amount of time producing detailed specifications that might be appropriate at the time of writing them, but might not actually add much value on the day of delivery. The window of opportunity for new systems is ever more dynamic and in many cases quite small or short, and so accurate valuable delivery is paramount.

1.2.2.3 Deliver working software frequently, from a couple of weeks to a couple of months, with a preference for the shorter timescale (see Section 10.2)

All Agile frameworks focus on delivering value-add product increments frequently, thereby enabling fast feedback-cycles and the ability to change direction if required. This means that Agile teams should deliver value-add stories to their customer every few weeks. Even when Agile is being scaled (see Section 14.8), and it may not be practical or feasible to deliver within a few weeks, teams should still try to deliver products in as short a period as possible – and never more than every few months.

A key metric that is therefore often implemented is 'cost of delay' (i.e. what is the cost to the business of delaying delivery of a product feature – see Section 10.1). This metric allows the customer to identify the opportunity cost of stories – meaning that they will be able to understand the relative cost of stories being available now, sooner or later.

1.2.2.4 Business people and developers must work together daily throughout the project (see Section 11.1)

In dynamic environments stories that add value and their relative priority will change as understanding evolves and business needs change. This constant 'reshuffling' requires close collaboration between the customers, stakeholders and team, as well as a common language, free from jargon. Face-to-face communication as well as a willingness to work together closely are key to creating this collaborative environment (see Section 8.2).

1.2.2.5 Build projects around motivated individuals. Give them the environment and support they need, and trust them to get the job done (see Section 9.1)

It is common sense that motivated people are going to be more productive (see Section 9.1). If an organisation treats people like robots who cannot be trusted, then the people will act like robots that cannot be trusted. If the organisation treats individuals like trusted adult professionals, then they will act in that way (see Section 9.1.2).

Agile can be extremely difficult if there is a blame culture, and/or when individuals and teams are not empowered. Agile transformation is an ongoing journey. Human beings will not transform unless they understand why they are transforming and what problems they are aiming to solve by implementing Agile.

1.2.2.6 The most efficient and effective method of conveying information to and within a development team is face-to-face communication (see Section 8.2)

Communication is not solely the spoken word – a significant amount comes from visual cues and body language. Therefore, written communication is prone to misunderstanding, and while documents and emails are a great way of broadcasting information, they are not a good communication tool.

If face-to-face communication is removed, feedback cycles can become unnecessarily and dangerously extended. Fast, frequent feedback cycles are essential in a dynamic environment (see Section 8.1) and can only really be provided through face-to-face communication.

Where teams are distributed geographically or even simply on different floors in a building it is important to implement a virtual collaboration/co-location environment, which is more than just video conferencing. The effective implementation of such an environment is the best, most suitable way to enable good (face-to-face) communication.

The importance of face-to-face communication is also why most Agile frameworks define individual development team sizes of somewhere between 3 and 11 people. This is not a new idea: the majority of teams across all human endeavours, including sports teams, emergency service teams, military units or any other teams that deliver in dynamic environments mainly consist of 3 to 11 people.

1.2.2.7 Working software is the primary measure of progress (see Section 10.3)

While there are many excellent ways to measure progress and quality, the main objective of Agile is to deliver value, i.e. working software, to the customer in short time frames continuously. This makes the delivery of working software the primary measure of progress.

1.2.2.8 Agile processes promote sustainable development. The sponsors, developers, and users should be able to maintain a constant pace indefinitely (see Section 6.2)

Agile teams must work at a sustainable pace (see Section 8) to avoid people burning out, becoming ill or experiencing stress-related conditions.

Unrealistic and unsustainable time pressures may also cause corner cutting, which can lead to 'technical debt' in a product (see Section 10.4). Technical debt describes the long-term effects of ignoring or not recognising functional or technical problems in a system, and tends to result in systems that are full of defects, not effectively documented and badly designed. These systems are therefore difficult, expensive and sometimes even impossible to support, maintain and enhance.

There may also come a point at which personal motivation and commitment to the team is lost, potentially resulting in people leaving the team and possibly even the business. Such losses can cost the team and the organisation a huge amount of money, as significant investment will have been made in that person and in their efforts.

The majority of Agile frameworks include a role called the Agile lead (see Section 6.3) who is responsible for ensuring that the teams are operating at a sustainable pace. This is to ensure that functional quality is built into products, that technical debt is kept out of products and that people do not leave unexpectedly.

1.2.2.9 Continuous attention to technical excellence and good design enhances agility (see Section 10.4)

If a team does not apply technical excellence and good design from the start, there is a significant chance that major problems will only be identified late in the delivery lifecycle, at which point they can become extremely expensive to fix. Allowing hacks (quick fixes that are not designed or implemented at a fit-for-purpose level of quality) to occur, or inappropriate design or architectures to creep in leads to technical debt (see Section 10.4).

This means that it is important that the team develop and build the right products in the right order in the optimum way. It is easy to deliver product stories without considering technical design holistically, but this will lead to a product that is fragile and unmaintainable; also, it will become increasingly difficult to develop product increments. If an area of a product is identified as being of a sub-standard design, the team should make sure that a 'refactoring' story (see Section 8.10) is raised to address this concern.

1.2.2.10 Simplicity – the art of maximising the amount of work not done – is essential (see Chapter 13)

Teams need to focus their efforts on developing a solution that is fit-for-purpose and only meets existing requirements. It is always tempting to build a product component that will meet current requirements, but is flexible enough to handle some perhaps-as-yet-undefined future requirement. However, this future requirement may never be needed or prioritised, which means the customer might end up with a product that is more expensive to maintain due to its complexity – which they didn't ask for or need.

It is equally important to concentrate on delivering value in the most effective way possible. This is where the concepts of Lean thinking (Liker, 2004) help to reduce waste and ensure the simplest 'value add' delivery chain possible is used (see Section 14.6).

1.2.2.11 The best architectures, requirements and designs emerge from self-organising teams (see Section 9.2)

With the right delivery environment and organisational culture a team can become self-organising (see Section 6.2), although this is not always a simple thing to achieve. For example, if detailed architectures, requirements and designs are defined without the team's input, there is the danger that the team will not buy into them, with the associated risk of loss of motivation. Agile assumes that teams typically know the best way forward at a detail level.

In more complex environments where many teams are working together to produce a product, it may be appropriate to produce high-level architectural and design principles.

Teams can then align to these principles, but will be responsible for producing the detailed architecture and design, typically with support from the people who created the architecture and design principles.

1.2.2.12 At regular intervals, the team reflects on how to become more effective, then tunes and adjusts its behaviour accordingly (see Section 11.2)

Agile deliveries follow an empirical process (i.e. a learning process – see Section 2.6). The three pillars of empirical processes are transparency, inspection and adaptation. Inspection and adaptation are of particular importance to this principle: at a frequent regular cadence, teams should take time to inspect their development process by reflecting on how things have progressed/developed since the last inspection and if there is anything that can be improved. Then these improvement ideas are used to adapt the development process.

This continuous improvement activity is known as a 'retrospective' (see Section 8.5). A retrospective will identify the areas and processes that work well, and those that need to be improved.

2 THE FOUNDATIONS OF AGILE

2.1 THE AGILE MINDSET

Figure 2.1 shows the different levels of Agile, from the tools and processes that operate within Agile practices, which in turn operate within Agile principles, up to everything operating within the Agile mindset. An Agile mindset implies that an organisation or person has absorbed Agile to the extent that it becomes part of their 'identity', i.e. their 'business-as-usual' state and the default way they interact with the world.

Figure 2.1 The Agile mindset wraps around everything

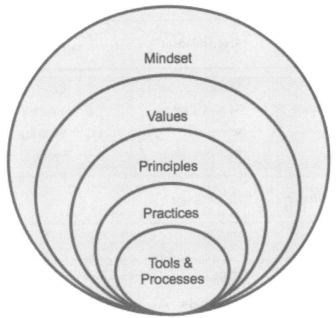

Agile is not about 'doing' Agile, it is about 'being Agile' and having an Agile mindset, and there are a number of tools, processes, practices and so on that facilitate this. An example could be:

Tool An Agile planning tool provides a visual board (see Section 8.7)

Practice Visual boards are common practice in most Agile frameworks

Principle The practice of using visual boards aligns to the empirical process principle of transparency (see Section 8.7)

Value The principle of transparency supports the Agile value of 'responding to change' (makes need for change and the resultant changes transparent)

Mindset All of these things are wrapped up in the Agile mindset

It is important to understand that, for Agile to be successful, the right mindset is equally, if not more, important than merely implementing Agile tools, practices or principles – for example, having a visual board does not necessarily mean that a team is Agile.

Experiments have shown that people can strongly influence each other to adopt or reject an Agile mindset (Dweck, 2012). Agile is a journey, not a destination and the best the organisation can hope for is that teams become more Agile by embedding the Agile mindset deeper inside themselves and the organisation. This process is facilitated by applying Agile values, practices, principles and so on.

Table 2.1 lists the characteristics of an Agile mindset and contrasts it with a non-Agile 'fixed' mindset (Rising, n.d.).

Table 2.1 Fixed and Agile mindsets

	Fixed mindset	**Agile mindset**
Ability	Static, like height	Can grow, like muscle
Goal	To look good	To learn
Challenge	Avoid	Embrace
Failure	Defines identity	Provides information
Effort	For those with no talent	Path to mastery
Reaction to challenge	Helplessness	Resilience

The most important aspect of an Agile mindset is understanding that Agile is neither just a set of rituals that are repeated, nor is it merely based on techniques.

2.1.1 Agile is not just a set of rituals

Sometimes, in an Agile transformation, the practices, principles, values and so on are only implemented with partial success. This can create a 'cargo cult' situation (see Box 2.1), where teams may understand what to do, but don't understand why they are doing it. If this happens teams tend to use Agile practices for a short period of time, but over the longer term they fall back into their previous ways of working, simply because they don't understand why they are doing what they are doing.

BOX 2.1 THE 'CARGO CULT' – AN EXAMPLE OF RITUALS

Some indigenous islanders on a South Sea island during the Second World War observed soldiers enabling parachute drops from an aircraft on an airfield that had been built on their island. To the islanders, it seemed like the military personnel signalled into the sky, and then food and equipment came from the sky.

In the mid-1970s, a long time after the airstrip had been decommissioned, a team of anthropologists visited the island. What they found was that an entire cult had been built around the idea of signalling into the sky in the hope that food would continue to fall out of it. This is actually a very logical thing to do based on an observation, however the South Sea Islanders had understood what to do but they hadn't understood why they were doing it.

Source: Feynman (1974)

2.1.2 Agile is not just techniques

People often prefer to pick out the elements of a framework they can easily understand rather than understanding an entire framework and why it should be implemented. This can lead to people equating the whole of an Agile framework with one or two individual elements of it and, inevitably, it will be difficult or even impossible to realise the whole benefits of implementing Agile. Some Agile frameworks (like Scrum – see Section 14.2) will only work effectively if all the key activities, roles and artefacts of the framework are in place.

So, for example, people might think that just prioritising stories within a backlog (see Section 7.1) is the same as 'being Agile', instead of it being just one part of the whole. Additionally, while prioritisation of stories is indeed a core practice in Agile, it is also used in more traditional non-Agile delivery approaches.

2.2 DELIVERY ENVIRONMENTS AND AGILE SUITABILITY

The environment within which delivery will occur should largely drive the delivery and governance framework(s) that will be implemented. For example, in a delivery environment where high variability is likely to be encountered (like IT product development), an Agile framework would be suited; in an environment where variability is likely to be low, a more defined process may be more suited (like 'Waterfall'). See below for more information.

2.2.1 Stacey's complexity model

Figure 2.2 illustrates an IT specialisation of a complexity model by Professor Ralph D. Stacey (Stacey, 1996). This model postulates that simple environments – from a perspective of the amount of variation and change they will experience – are those where customer and team have agreed requirements and the technology is close to certainty early within the delivery cycle.

Figure 2.2 Stacey's complexity model

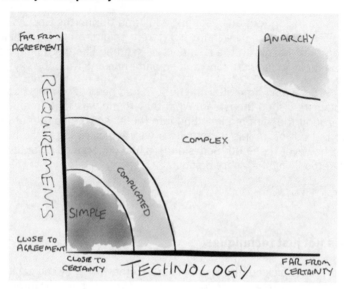

In a simple environment it is possible to use a defined process, which expects the requirements, technology, design and so on to be largely defined before moving onto the next stage. The Waterfall model (see Section 2.6.3) is an example of a defined process. This means that in some instances what appears to be a very complex project, such as building a bridge, may actually be in the simple area because it may not experience a lot of requirements or technology variation through the delivery lifecycle.

In contrast, in complicated, complex or anarchic environments it is important to use an empirical (learning) process where product increments are developed frequently and consistently in order to obtain feedback and to make sure that the finished product aligns with the evolving business environment. Agile frameworks are empirical processes (see Section 2.6).

Most modern knowledge-work environments (like IT) are likely to fall into the complicated, complex or anarchic areas because, by their nature, they tend to be innovative and operate in environments where requirements and technology have a high degree of variability through the delivery lifecycle. This is reflected in the Agile frameworks that have been developed for these types of environments: they are empirical and enable teams to run experiments, observe and understand the results, and then adapt processes as appropriate to improve the certainty and quality of delivery.

When trying to understand types of environments, it is important to take into account the amount of innovation that is being sought or considered for a new product or service. As the level of innovation increases, so does the move towards complexity, and a high variability is likely to be present.

2.2.2 Cynefin framework

The Cynefin framework (Snowdon and Boone, 2007; Figure 2.3) gives an alternative framework for determining and understanding simple, complicated and complex environments.

Figure 2.3 Cynefin framework

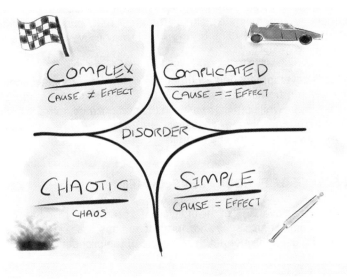

Cynefin identifies five domains:

- **Simple (obvious) domain** In this domain the relationship between cause and effect is obvious and therefore it is relatively easy to predict an outcome. In this domain predictive planning works well as everything is pretty well understood. Teams can define up front how best to deliver a product, and they can then create a defined approach and plan. The Waterfall model works well in these types of environments with little variability.

- **Complicated domain** In this domain, the relationship between cause and effect becomes less obvious; however, after a period of analysis it should generally be possible to come up with a defined approach and plan. Such a plan will normally include contingency to take into account the fact that the analysis may be flawed by a certain amount. Again, the Waterfall model is suitable for this environment as there is an element of definition up front; however, a more empirical process, like Agile, may be more suited.

- **Complex domain** In this domain the relationship between cause and effect starts to break down as there tend to be many different factors that drive the effect. While it may be possible to identify retrospectively a relationship between cause and effect, the cause of an effect today may be different to the cause of the same effect tomorrow. Creating a defined up-front approach and plan is not effective within this domain and therefore an Agile way of working is recommended.

- **Chaotic domain** In this domain, there is no recognisable relationship between cause and effect at all, making it impossible to define an approach up front or to plan at all. Instead, teams must perform experiments (e.g. prototyping, modelling) with the aim to move into one of the other less chaotic domains. An Agile approach can work in this domain, for example Kanban (see Section 14.5), which does not require up-front plans.

- **Disorder** Being in this environment means that it is impossible to determine which domain definition applies. This is the most risky domain as teams tend to fall into their default way of working, which may prove unsuitable for what they are trying to achieve.

During a product's development and evolution there may be elements of delivery spread across all the Cynefin domains at the same time. There may be aspects of a large system that are simple, while others may be in the complicated domain; and there could also be areas where innovation is necessary and which require a move towards the complex or even towards the chaotic domain.

2.3 THE LIFECYCLE OF PRODUCT DEVELOPMENT

This section will give an overview of the lifecycle of a product from initial commissioning to final decommissioning and discuss how project and business-as-usual (BAU) delivery frameworks may be used throughout the lifecycle of the product (see Figure 2.4).

Figure 2.4 The lifecycle of product development

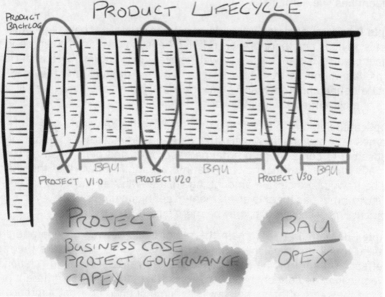

The full lifetime of any product spans from the commissioning of the product to its decommissioning. Depending on the business that is implementing the product this could be anything from a few weeks or months (a short marketing campaign), to many decades (a bank's accounting system).

What drives product development in an Agile approach is an evolving backlog of stories (see Section 7.1) that the customer wants and that are placed in an order by the customer. The backlog exists throughout the whole product lifetime, from commissioning to decommissioning. The customer evolves the backlog with the stakeholders and the team. Typically the stakeholders support the customer to define coarse-grained stories in the backlog and the team supports the customer to define fine-grained stories in the backlog.

There are generally three styles of Agile delivery:

- Defined product via a BAU delivery – This style assumes that the customer wants a high-level definition of the product and will assign funding and resources over a time frame to deliver that product, which may or may not be defined in a business case. The team and customer will evolve the product within the available timescale and resources, prioritising what will be delivered.

- Defined product via a project delivery – This style assumes that the customer wants a high-level definition of the product and will assign funding and resources over a time frame; however, the complexity of delivery (or preference of the customer) means project governance will be in place. Projects must have a business case. The team and customer will evolve the product within the available timescale and resources governed within a project framework to monitor delivery against a business case.

- Undefined product via a BAU delivery – This style of delivery assumes that the customer doesn't have an end point definition of a product or specific timescale or cost in mind up front. The customer and team will define what increment of the product they want in the next iteration/sprint and then create that increment. Once that increment has been delivered the next delivery increment is planned and delivered in the next iteration/sprint. The delivery continues until funding runs out or it doesn't make sense to evolve the product any further. This creates an environment where delivery can be extremely flexible and emergent, which is excellent for highly variable delivery environments. Arguably this style of delivery is the nearest to what some people may consider to be 'pure Agile'.

Whichever style of Agile is being applied (and it may be all of them across different teams) a key focus of Agile is enabling effective product flow, which will therefore enable continuous delivery of value to the customer. Effective product flow is enabled by many factors, one of which is batch size. Projects and releases can lead to large batch sizes which in turn can lead to, amongst other problems, errors and low productivity (see Section 10.1.1). Therefore, when implementing Agile the delivery sprints/iterations (batch sizes) should be as small as possible (2 to 4 weeks is typical), and shippable product should be produced at the end of each sprint/iteration. Grouping iterations/ sprints into releases or projects can lead to large batch sizes, which is sub-optimal, however there may be strong business reasons (like the customer only wanting quarterly deliveries) why this must happen. Agile people talk about 'potentially shippable increments' to deal with this issue.

There is sometimes confusion about whether project management frameworks can or should be wrapped around Agile frameworks. This is often due to a fundamental misunderstanding of what project management frameworks are, and concerns that the frameworks will be delivered in a 'command and control' style that will stifle agility. However, all project management frameworks – including PRINCE2 (Projects IN Controlled Environments (Axelos, 2014)) and PMBoK (Project Management Body of Knowledge (PMI)) – are designed to wrap around many other frameworks, including Agile frameworks; however, they must be customised.

As an example, PRINCE2 consists of seven guiding principles. The seventh principle guides users to customise their delivery approach depending on the environment in which it will be used:

> PRINCE2 is tailored to suit the project's environment, size, complexity, importance, capability and risk.
>
> (Axelos, 2014)

Therefore when using PRINCE2 with Agile, PRINCE2 should be customised for the Agile environment. So, for example, the 'Manage Stage Boundary' milestones in PRINCE2, which are aligned in a Waterfall delivery to end of analysis, end of design, end of build and so on, will, when integrated with an Agile framework, actually relate to delivery of outcomes at release boundaries, and not to Waterfall stage gates and documents. This means what will be assessed is the delivery of outcomes, rather than the delivery of products associated with the Waterfall stages.

If a project management framework is required in conjunction with an Agile framework that does not provide its own project governance, there is a standard Agile framework that has been designed to wrap around other Agile frameworks. This is called 'AgilePM' (Agile Project Management – see Section 14.4) which is part of the 'DSDM Agile Project Framework' (see Section 14.3).

2.4 THE 'IRON TRIANGLE'

The 'Iron Triangle' (see Figure 2.5) is a means to show the constraints that need to be kept in mind when developing products as changes in one constraint affect the others. The traditional primary constraints are features (requirements), time and cost, but we have added technical quality as a fourth constraint. In a delivery, teams and customers have to choose which particular constraint(s) they wish to fix, if indeed they fix any of them, and which ones they want to keep as dynamic elements. This section will discuss broadly how Waterfall and Agile approaches fix and vary the constraints of the Iron Triangle.

2.4.1 The Waterfall implementation of the Iron Triangle

The Iron Triangle on the left in Figure 2.5 above shows a traditional Waterfall approach (see Section 2.6.3), where all features are defined (and possibly fixed) up front and a project is planned up front to deliver all of those predefined features. Therefore in the Waterfall Iron Triangle the features are largely fixed and become part of an actual or implied contract between the customer and the team. The assumption is that quality, time and cost will be the variable elements. This approach works well for deliveries

Figure 2.5 The 'Iron Triangle'

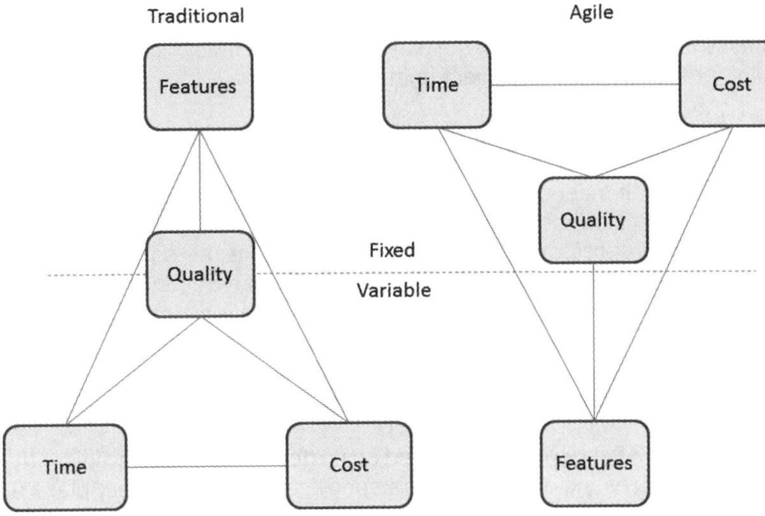

where the feature requirements and/or technology are simple and unlikely to change (the simple area in Stacey's model – see Section 2.2.1).

However, this approach can cause problems if operating in an environment that experiences variability. For example, if the features are set pre-delivery, they become the fixed point on the triangle. If the customer then needs to change what they want or if the up-front analysis and design prove to be incorrect, potentially expensive and invasive change control has to be introduced, meaning that time and cost may grow significantly.

Most organisations need IT solutions to be delivered on time, simply because IT is such a significant enabler of competitive business advantage. Therefore when things start to vary, expand or go wrong, the business needs to find a way to bring the project back on schedule. In a traditional Waterfall model, where the features are fixed there is a risk that this is done by simply adding more people to the development team. This, in turn, introduces the potential for increased risk, cost and complexity.

There have been many white papers and books written about the risks of simply throwing people at a project that is experiencing delivery problems. One of the fundamental problems of this approach is that the people who are already in the project team will need to spend significant unplanned time and effort on bringing people who are new to the team up to speed. This will typically cause time to slip further.

Probably the most famous book that discusses this is *The Mythical Man-Month* (Brooks, 1995), which asserts that adding manpower to a late software project just makes it even later (Brooks' law).

It describes the sequence of problematic events as follows:

- A time delay leads to more people, and the associated costs, to be added to the project.

19

- Bringing those people up to speed causes further time delay (because of the 'learning curve'), so leading to more people and more associated costs being added to the project to bring it back on schedule.

- This causes further time delay, so the team add more people and the associated... and so on until a very costly project failure.

Another significant risk of using a Waterfall approach in a dynamic environment is the possible effect on quality. If the features change, quality might be squeezed or even ignored in an attempt to meet the all-important delivery date. For example testing might be shortened and de-prioritised, architectures and designs may be compromised, and possibly detrimental shortcuts may be allowed to 'make the software work' in the immediate term, eventually leading to technical debt (see Section 10.4). This can be exacerbated by the difficulty of changing detailed specifications that have been created pre-delivery.

2.4.2 The Agile implementation of the Iron Triangle

On the right of Figure 2.5 the triangle is turned on its head; this is the paradigm that Agile creates. Rather than creating detailed feature specifications and delivery plans up front, Agile fixes the time, as well as cost and quality, which enables the features to be reviewed and evolved to stay in line with the dynamic needs of contemporary businesses.

2.4.2.1 Time-boxing

This concept is called 'time-boxing'. Time-boxing divides the delivery of increments of the product into short, manageable time periods (called sprints or iterations) of days or weeks, and varies, based on priority, the functionality to be delivered within these time-boxes. While quality can still be changed, the focus is always on understanding the risk of adding technical debt by changing the quality.

A project is a time-box, a release is a shorter time-box, and an iteration/sprint is an even shorter time-box, and all of these can be controlled effectively by Agile. The goal related to the iteration/sprint time-box is a commitment, whereas the goals related to project and release time-boxes are baselines, which can be changed.

Sceptics sometimes wrongly criticise Agile projects for not defining what is going to be delivered up front. They think that an Agile project delivers 'something' within a time frame and that the development team 'make it up' as they go along – these are incorrect assumptions. It may be true that in a highly variable/chaotic environment the only way to deliver something is on an increment-by-increment basis within very short planning horizons of iterations/sprints. However, typically Agile incorporates a short and effective up-front period of time for set-up work as and where required – for example, in Scrum (Section 14.2) there is a 'Sprint Zero'; in eXtreme Programming (see Section 14.1), there is an 'Iteration Zero'; and in Agile Project Management and DSDM (see Section 14.3) there are 'Feasibility' and 'Foundation' stages.

Set-up normally requires a couple of weeks in which a high-level understanding of the vision of the project is achieved, together with a high-level prototype and a high-level technical architecture. These need to be short enough to be accurate and simple enough to be changed effectively and without huge overspend.

2.5 WORKING WITH UNCERTAINTY AND VOLATILITY

Early in an Agile delivery little is generally known about the work needed. At this stage, any estimates have higher uncertainty and thus are often provided using a range or with contingencies and the associated costs.

As the delivery progresses and knowledge increases, the level of variation in estimates is reduced to the point when more and more accurate forecasts can be provided. Boehm's Cone of Uncertainty (Boehm, 1981) (see Figure 2.6) explains the relationship between the level of knowledge and the amount of uncertainty that should be expected in providing any estimate based on effort, cost and/or time.

Figure 2.6 Boehm's Cone of Uncertainty

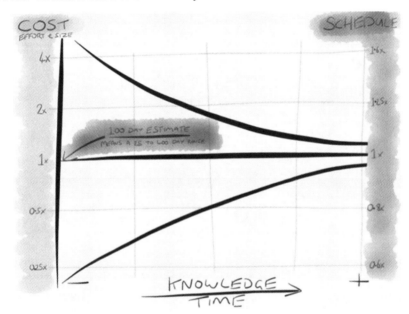

The traditional Waterfall model is based in part on the belief that doing significant amounts of analysis and design will create a deep understanding and knowledge of the system. However, this fails to take into account the inherent uncertainty and variability in knowledge-based work such as software delivery.

Accurate knowledge can only be reasonably acquired by interacting with a tangible product as it is delivered. Therefore, the more opportunities the team, customers and stakeholders have to experience the product collaboratively, the more opportunity they have to discuss and agree the evolving product requirements and technology needs, and therefore the more accurate their evolving estimates will be.

2.6 EMPIRICAL AND DEFINED PROCESSES

2.6.1 The three pillars of the empirical process

Agile product development follows an empirical process (a learning process).The three pillars of empirical processes are (see Figure 2.7):

Figure 2.7 Three pillars of empirical processes

- Inspection – inspect the product being created and how it is being created
- Adaptation – adapt the product being created or the creation process if required
- Transparency – ensure everyone can easily see what is happening

People use empirical processes in their daily lives. It is the way people learn most effectively, i.e. learning through experience and from mistakes (Bryner, 2007).

In an empirical process the team inspect the environment in which they are delivering (see Section 2.2), and then adapt what they are doing and how they are doing it to suit the environment. If the team are going to 'inspect and adapt' then they need to make sure that the adaptation is transparent to all stakeholders (see Section 6.4).

2.6.2 Empirical processes

Empirical processes (see Figure 2.8) incorporate repeated inspection and adaptation of a product to ensure the right product is delivered in the right way. This is especially important in environments that experience high variability (see Section 2.2) and are therefore most suited to Agile working.

Figure 2.8 Empirical change model

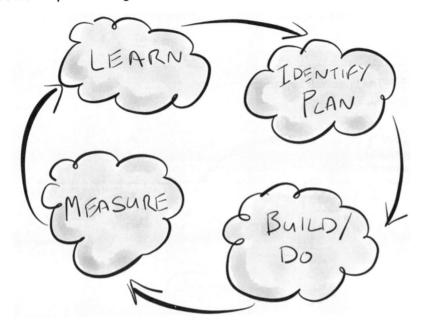

There are many Agile frameworks (see Chapter 14), however, they all have a similar underlying structure in that they identify something that needs to be done, do it, measure and review the results, and then inspect and adapt based on that knowledge. Some examples of empirical models are as follows:

PDCA Plan, Do, Check, Act – Edward Deming (Deming, n.d.).

POOGI Process of On-Going Improvement – Theory of Constraints (Goldratt and Cox, 1984).

OODA Observe, Orient, Decide, Act – John Boyd (Boyd, n.d.).

BML Build, Measure, Learn – Lean Start-up (Ries, 2011).

DMAIC Define, Measure, Analyse, Improve, Control (Six Sigma, 2006).

TAC Thought, Action, Conversation – DSDM Agile Project Framework (DSDM Consortium, 2014b).

Kaizen A Japanese word which means 'good change', used to describe a philosophy of continuous improvement (Liker, 2004).

2.6.3 Defined processes

One of the best-known defined processes is the Waterfall approach (see Figure 2.9). The Waterfall approach was originally implemented in the civil engineering environment. In these environments the cost of change is typically prohibitive and therefore it makes great sense to define exactly what is required (requirements and analysis), design exactly what is required (design), build it (build), test it works and meets requirements (test), and then make it operational.

Figure 2.9 The Waterfall approach

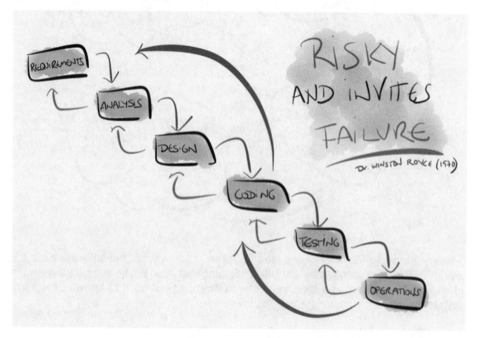

The Waterfall approach was also one of the first formal delivery approaches utilised by the IT industry. It was first cited as an example of how software **could** be delivered by Dr Winston Royce in an article titled *Managing the development of large software systems* in 1970 (Royce, 1987[1970]), although Royce didn't use the term Waterfall. He also stated, 'I believe in this concept, but the implementation described above is risky and invites failure' (Royce, 1987[1970]). Many IT people read Royce's paper, saw the Waterfall diagram and implemented it, but missed Royce's warning about using it as described in the diagram.

The arguments for the Waterfall style of delivery are as follows:

- Effort spent analysing and designing up front will lead to greater understanding and also lead to a solution that is less likely to contain errors.

- Ensuring that each stage is rigorously completed will ensure that problems will not occur later in the delivery when they are very costly to fix.

- Communication is via documentation, which ensures that if anyone leaves there will not be a significant impact on the delivery.

- Waterfall implements rigour and predictability via detailed delivery stages that are signed off as milestones.

These arguments are all very robust in a simple domain (see Section 2.2.2). However, in environments like IT where the cost of change is not prohibitive and variability is high, the Waterfall approach does not work effectively due to it not being designed for these environments.

3 AGILE AND THE BUSINESS

3.1 THE ECONOMIC CASE FOR AGILE

Agile is focused on delivering value to the business within the shortest effective time frame, and so enable businesses to achieve a positive return on investment as soon as possible. This creates a very compelling economic case; the more Agile a business is, the easier it is for the business to change direction and understand the implications of doing so on an as-and-when-needed basis. This ability is essential in today's fast evolving markets with their ever-decreasing windows of opportunity, and in businesses where IT is a key enabler and differentiator.

There are many ways to measure delivery economics. One of the most effective that is used regularly in Agile deliveries is product flow economic modelling. This approach recommends that many economic variables should be considered when deciding the order of delivery, however, if only one thing is going to be measured, it should be cost of delay (the cost to the business of not implementing a feature at a point in time – for example, losing competitive advantage). We will look at this in more detail in Section 10.1.

In the following we will look at some of the surveys and studies that have been published to help make an economic case for Agile.

3.1.1 The Chaos Manifesto 2011

The Chaos Manifesto 2011 from the Standish Group (Standish, 2002) identified the following figures in relation to project success, comparing Waterfall against Agile product deliveries (see Table 3.1).

Table 3.1 Standish Chaos Manifesto 2011

	Successful	Challenged	Failed
Waterfall	14%	57%	29%
Agile	42%	49%	9%

Figures from Standish database 2002 to 2010

The report says:

> The Agile process is the universal remedy for software development project failure. Software applications developed through the Agile process have three times the success rate of the traditional Waterfall method and a much lower percentage of time and cost overruns.
>
> (Standish, 2002)

'Success' is defined as on time, on budget and with all planned features. There is no indication of how many deliveries were assessed, however, the assessment period was between 2001 and 2010.

3.1.2 The Cutter Consortium report 2008

The Cutter Consortium report entitled 'How Agile projects measure up, and what this means to you' by Mah and Lunt (2008) provides an exhaustive insight into the impact that the adoption of Agile had on the IT industry, especially when considering scaled Agile. The report analysed a database of 7,500 completed Waterfall-driven IT projects and then compared key measures (e.g. cost and time) against 20 Agile releases from five different companies. The results showed that two of the companies achieved best-in-class levels of performance from using Agile.

Company 1 used a collocated eXtreme Programming approach (XP – see Section 14.1). Table 3.2 shows that it ran teams that were broadly the same size as industry average for this size of project, yet it achieved some very significant benefits.

Company 2 used a distributed Scrum approach (see Section 14.2). It wanted to ensure fast time to market for their product and therefore their team size was larger than the industry average. While there are significant risks with increasing team size to enable speed time to market (see Section 2.4.1), the numbers show that their Agile approach

Table 3.2 Cutter Consortium – example 1

	Company 1		
	Industry average	Agile delivery	Improvement (%)
Cost ($m)	3.5	2.2	37
Schedule (months)	12.6	7.8	38
Defects (at QA)	242	121	50
Staff	35	35	n/a

Using average project size on 500K lines of code

Source: Mah and Lunt (2008)

enabled Company 2 to implement a team significantly larger than average but also achieve significant improvement in time to market whilst delivering fewer defects and lower costs than average (see Table 3.3).

Table 3.3 Cutter Consortium – example 2

	Company 2		
	Industry average	**Agile delivery**	**Improvement (%)**
Cost ($m)	5.5	5.2	5
Schedule (months)	15	6.3	58
Defects (at QA)	713	635	11
Staff	40	92	n/a

Using average project size on 700K lines of code

Source: Mah and Lunt (2008)

3.1.3 State of Agile survey

Another often quoted source of Agile economic statistics is the annual 'State of Agile' survey produced by VersionOne (VersionOne, n.d.; Table 3.4). These statistics are based on input from a global community of Agile practitioners who are asked how they rate the importance of Agile to achieve certain objectives. Although this doesn't directly support the economic case for Agile, it does give an indication of how relatively important survey respondents think Agile is to achieving key objectives like time to market.

Table 3.4 State of Agile survey 2013

	Not important	**Somewhat important**	**Very important**	**Most important**
Time to market	3	21	43	32
Managing priorities	3	17	54	27
Better alignment IT/business	9	27	42	23
Increase productivity	3	24	55	19
Increase software quality	6	28	48	18
Reduce risk	6	35	47	12
Reduce cost	15	40	35	10

3.2 BUSINESS CULTURE AND AGILE

Business culture is what defines the business. It can be seen in things such as organisation charts, role descriptions, processes and tools, but is really defined by how people interact with each other, and the customs, beliefs, stereotypes, values and taboos in an organisation – all of which are typically much harder to recognise and visualise.

Understanding the dominant culture of a business is a fundamental exercise before embarking on any Agile transformation, simply because the existing dominant culture may present a serious obstacle to implementing an Agile approach. 'Culture models' can help to visualise and determine a business's culture and to understand how it may hinder or help the implementation of an Agile approach.

One such model is the Schneider culture change model (Schneider, 1999; Figure 3.1). It defines 'culture' as the answer to the question: 'How do we do things here to succeed?' Based on the answer, it describes four distinct cultures:

Figure 3.1 Schneider culture change model

CULTURE = "How we do things around here to succeed."

"The Reengineering Alternative." William Schneider

REALITY (Actuality) ORIENTED

"We succeed by working together."

Affiliation   Synergy

COLLABORATION

Partnership

Trust

Interaction   People

Teams   Diversity

Egalitarian

"We succeed by getting and keeping control."

POWER

CONTROL   Predictability

SECURITY

Standardization   Hierarchical

Stability   Order

Process

PEOPLE ORIENTED

COMPANY ORIENTED

(Personal) "We succeed by growing people who fulfil our vision."

(Impersonal)

"We succeed by being the best."

Efficiency   Professionalism

CULTIVATION   GROW↑

COMPETENCE

Purpose/Faith   Dedication

Meritocracy   Achievement

Let things Evolve   Subjectivity

Craftsmanship   Expertise   Creativity   Be the Best

Creativity

POSSIBILITY ORIENTED

cc Agilitrix 2011

- **Collaboration** culture is about working together.
- **Control** culture is about getting and keeping control.
- **Competence** culture is about being the best.
- **Cultivation** culture is about learning and growing with a sense of purpose.

The axes of the model define whether the business is more people or company oriented and whether the business is more focused on today's realities or on tomorrow's possibilities.

Michael Spayd undertook a culture survey of Agilistas (Spayd, 2011). His landmark results show that Agile practitioners have a particular culture profile and identified the key elements as collaboration and cultivation. The results suggest that Agile is all about the people. Interestingly, the survey included Scrum, XP, as well as Kanban software practitioners (see Figure 3.2).

Michael Sahota then mapped the Agile manifesto values and principles to the Schneider model (Sahota, 2012) which showed there is high density of values and practices that are aligned with collaboration and cultivation. There were no elements related to control culture and only one related to competence culture. So both Sahota's and Spayd's analysis were strikingly similar.

Figure 3.2 Schneider culture change model – Agile friendly

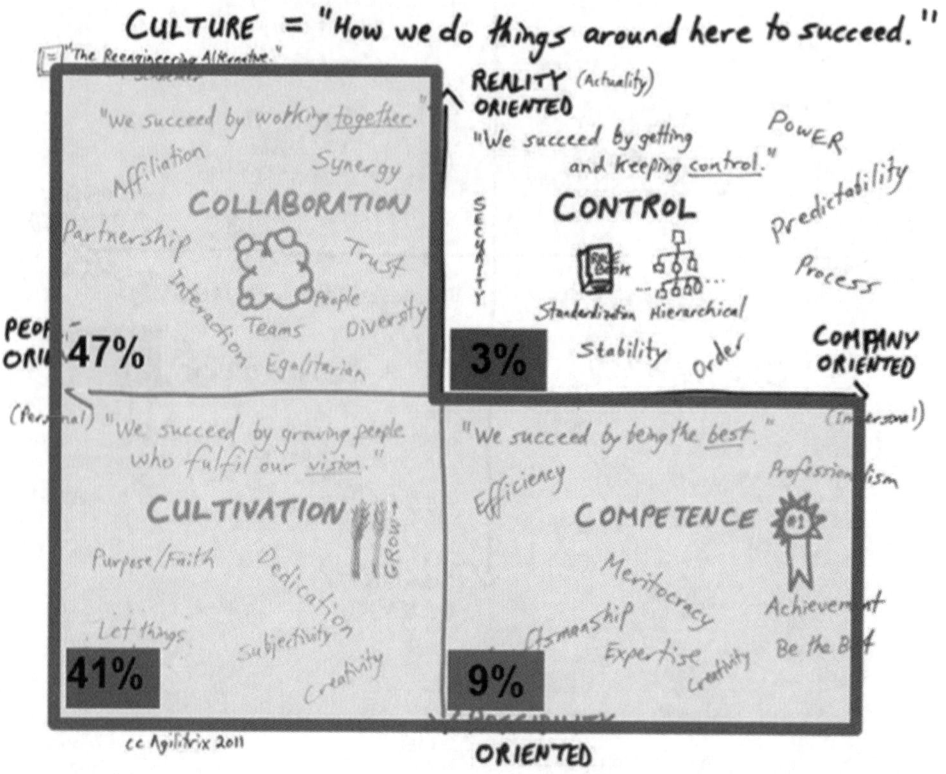

3.2.1 The 'journey to agility'

A significant part of any Agile transformation is enabling an organisation to move away from a command and control culture to an environment that is more focused on collaboration and cultivation (see Figure 3.3). This creates an environment in which teams can focus on delivering products of the appropriate level of quality whilst self-organising.

Figure 3.3 Schneider culture change model – journey to agility

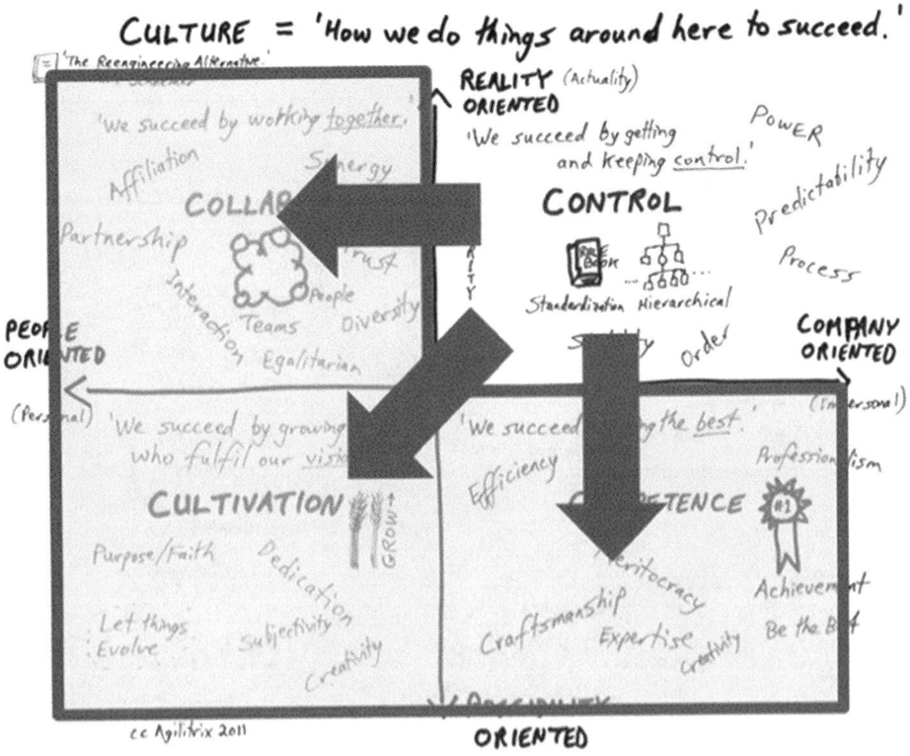

Creating an Agile business culture requires the team, as well as the people around the team, to buy into Agile values and principles. This includes key stakeholders, customers and the management team as it can prove very difficult, if not impossible, for an Agile approach to work effectively if the people around the team aren't (yet) aligned.

A key role to help this transformation is that of the Agile lead (see Section 6.3). They are responsible for helping team members make the cultural shift from command and control and to cultivate collaboration. In addition, they also work with stakeholders, customers and management teams to help them understand the Agile principles and values that are necessary to create a culture in which the team can inspect and adapt with support and confidence.

Cultural change is fundamentally important to any transformation, and arguably even more so with Agile where the mindset change is so significant (see Section 2.1). Trying to implement any transformation without taking into consideration the cultural aspect of a business is a fatal mistake that inevitably leads to failure.

Figure 3.4 illustrates a situation where the visible formal system of an organisation has been changed without the underlying culture being changed and aligned. Training the team members, changing their job titles and implementing new processes and tools are not sufficient to create a sustainable transformation to Agile. A significant amount of time and money can typically be spent/wasted changing the visible formal system, which will then inevitably sink back into the ocean because it is not supported by the culture of the business.

Figure 3.4 The organisational iceberg

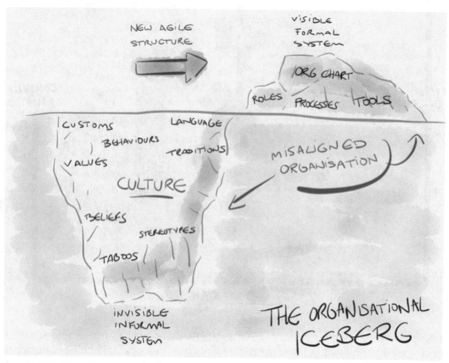

(Source: Plant, 1989)

4 AGILE MYTHS

As with any framework or method, myths and misunderstandings can gain credence and become 'common knowledge' over time. This chapter discusses common myths that many people associate with Agile and explains why they are just myths and not facts.

MYTH: AGILE IS NEW

Agile is certainly not new. Agile methods have been around for a long time. The frameworks that collectively are now known as 'Agile' mainly evolved in the late 1980s and 1990s, which means that Agile is mature and an approach that is inherently familiar to most people. In essence Agile is all about enabling inspection and adaptation in dynamic environments where variability is experienced. This is a founding principle of complexity theory, chaos theory and evolutionary theory. It is also the way human beings interact with the world on a day-to-day basis – indeed it is the only way human beings can interact effectively with a complicated and complex world.

MYTH: IMPLEMENTING AGILE IS EASY

This common misunderstanding is the single biggest challenge when endeavouring to implement Agile delivery capabilities in an organisation or team. While Agile frameworks are inherently simple, the effort needed to implement an effective Agile operating model (see Section 5.1) is not as it requires cultural change. It is usually not easy to change a complex systems delivery lifecycle (SDLC) to a simple one; organisations normally find it easier to make things more complex than to simplify them.

Sadly, what happens in some organisations is that they try to implement an Agile operating model or a single Agile framework 'by the book' and without understanding the transformational complexity. Therefore they either fail to implement Agile, or they do achieve some success but at significantly higher cost and pain than they would have done if they had managed the transformation more effectively. Such organisations inevitably fail to achieve the true benefits of Agile. You can theoretically learn to fly a plane by reading a book, but don't expect me to sit next to you on your first take-off!

MYTH: AGILE GIVES INSTANT BENEFIT

While a transformation to Agile can deliver huge benefits, the reality is that the majority of transformations go through a 'learning curve'. Whilst people and organisations are learning, the delivery capability can actually go downwards before it makes the step-change upwards and begins to achieve the new improved delivery capability.

MYTH: AGILE MEANS NO DOCUMENTATION

This myth most likely stems from a misinterpretation of the Agile Manifesto where it states 'We value working software over comprehensive documentation'. It is important to understand that the Manifesto does **not** say that documentation is not required, it says that the focus is on producing working software instead of spending exhaustive amounts of time creating detailed documentation up front.

All effective Agile deliveries should allow for and produce focused, value-driven, business-beneficial documentation that enables the business to use the product effectively and the technical team to support and maintain it. Failing to produce appropriate documentation would be a classic example of technical debt (see Section 10.4.1).

MYTH: AGILE MEANS 'HACKING' CODE TOGETHER WITH LITTLE THOUGHT OR DESIGN

'Hacking' in Agile means 'cobbling together' an IT system with little or any design or architectural thinking.

The Agile Manifesto (see Section 1.2) states that 'Continuous attention to technical excellence and good design enhances agility' and many Agile frameworks provide the tools and techniques for the team to produce very high quality code. For example, in eXtreme Programming (XP – see Section 14.1), many practices are aimed specifically at ensuring that the quality of the product being delivered is fit for purpose. This includes the practice of 'Pair Programming', where developers work in pairs to help each other write the best designed software assets that can be created (see Section 14.1.4). This provides constant quality assurance (QA) and leads to continuous refactoring (see Section 8.10.1), a technique used to increase robustness and simplification of the design of the system without changing the behaviour of the system.

Many Agile teams subscribe to the concepts of 'Software Craftsmanship' (McBreen, 2002). A software craftsman creates easy-to-understand software that is designed well, documented well and is easy to build on in the future. In this context it is also important to understand that, in an Agile development, one of the main results should be the delivery of functionally and technically fit-for-purpose products. This means that it is perfectly acceptable for an Agile team to reduce the quality level for a tactical product that does not require high quality.

MYTH: AGILE IS A 'SILVER BULLET'

Agile is not the answer to all IT problems. There is no single answer to all IT problems; rather it's about integrating different frameworks that each provides part of the answer. The implementation of delivery and management frameworks such as Agile must be pragmatic. It must recognise the real-world environment in which a system will be implemented and used, and consider the best integration of Agile and non-Agile frameworks that will work in that real-world environment – there is no single 'silver bullet' framework.

This means that, once a team or an organisation has implemented something that works effectively, which will typically be a pragmatic mix of different delivery and management frameworks, it should then continuously evolve this to further increase capability within the changing business environment. This concept is known as 'Kaizen' (continuous improvement) in Lean (Liker, 2004) (see Section 2.6.2).

MYTH: AGILE – JUST READ A BOOK

Understanding Agile is not something that can be achieved by simply reading a book. It is a very good idea to select some of the Agile books from the leading Agile exponents and read those; however, just reading a book cannot replace the practical experience that is essential to enabling an Agile mindset (see Section 2.1) and successfully transforming an organisation or team to become Agile.

This book serves as a fundamentals-level introduction to Agile, and we have referenced many other sources that we believe will help the reader on their Agile journey. However, as in most things, there is no substitute for practical experience.

MYTH: AGILE ONLY RELATES TO SOFTWARE DELIVERY

It is true that the Agile Manifesto describes Agile within the context of software delivery, but Agile can be applied successfully in business environments that are not exclusively software-related. In essence, Agile is suited to any dynamic business environment that experiences variability (e.g. marketing, business change and so on).

MYTH: AGILE SHOULD REPLACE EVERYTHING ALL AT ONCE ('BIG BANG' TRANSFORMATION)

When Agile is applied in a big-bang approach across large projects, programmes or across the entire organisation, there is a significant risk that the benefits of an Agile operating model (see Section 5.1) will not be realised or understood. Often the organisation and its staff will simply continue to do things as they have always done them while pretending – or believing – that they have moved to an Agile method.

Transforming capability is a long-term process of learning and change. Businesses evolve and the best way to do business evolves. It is therefore a mistake to implement a 'big-bang' Agile transformation and then just assume further improvement is no longer necessary.

Effective transformation is all about visualisation; a typical successful Agile transformation first transforms a vertical slice (i.e. a deliverable part of the overall system conceptualised as a 'slice' across the data, business rules and user interface (UI) layers of the architecture – see Section 13.2.1) of the entire target delivery organisation. It then measures and proves the effectiveness of the Agile approach before endeavouring to transform the remainder of the organisation. Without this tangible, factual, organisational visualisation it can be very difficult to get anyone to realistically transform.

In certain circumstances there may be a requirement for a big-bang transformation, for example, if an organisation's competitors are already Agile, which may make competing with them very difficult or impossible. However, this is relatively rare and needs high-quality support from experienced transformational Agile leads.

There is an interesting quote, which is generally attributed to Albert Einstein; it's referred to as Einstein's definition of insanity...

Insanity is doing the same thing over and over and expecting a different result.

This statement nicely sums up failed Agile transformations where the organisation is still doing exactly what they have done previously (i.e. 'W'Agile – 'Waterfall pretending to be Agile'), and expecting added value even though they haven't actually changed anything.

MYTH: AGILE MEANS NO PLANNING – 'JUST DO IT'

The vast majority of Agile frameworks involve frequent, regular and evolutionary planning (see Section 7.3).

If a team is largely doing maintenance work or defect fixing (BAU work), or there is no need for the customer to look any further than a couple of weeks when creating a product, they will probably only be planning in single iterations/sprints.

If the customer does need to know roughly what product will be delivered within what timescale and at what cost, the team may be planning in releases containing iterations/sprints (one way to do this is by using 'Agile release trains' – see Section 14.8).

If there are 'release plans', a high-level agreement will be in place of what product is being delivered, and at what timescale and cost. However, the agreement and the plans are specifically set up to enable change, and there will be significant frequent, regular ongoing planning.

If the customer needs to get an understanding of the total baseline definition of a product within a baseline time and cost, then this could be delivered in multiple releases or an Agile project. If an Agile project is initiated, then high-level baseline definitions of the product and plans will be required; however, these are purposefully left at a high level as it is assumed that things will change as more is understood about the product.

Agile isn't 'just do it'; there is significant planning and re-planning involved when required.

PART 2
A GENERIC AGILE FRAMEWORK

It is not our intention to create another Agile framework in this part of the book. There are now many Agile frameworks that can be integrated very successfully to satisfy most situations where Agile may be suitable; this is described further in Section 5.1.

The Agile frameworks described in Chapter 14 represent what we consider to be (arguably) the most popular frameworks in the Agile world (we define 'popular' as the frameworks we have seen most implemented in organisations we have interacted with over the last 16 years). These frameworks have been used and integrated successfully over many years and many of these can now be considered to be standards.

As these standard frameworks all overlap and often use different terminology to describe the same thing, this part of the book covers the main products, processes and roles in a generalised Agile process based on the framework standards. It provides a synopsis of what the Agile frameworks cover and a generic language to ease understanding of the rest of the book.

5   GENERIC AGILE PROCESS

This chapter describes a generic integrated Agile process and terminology based on the standard Agile frameworks (see Chapter 14).

A brief chronological overview of the generic Agile process is displayed in Figure 5.1 (scaled Agile is not considered in any detail) and outlined below:

Figure 5.1 Simplified generic Agile process

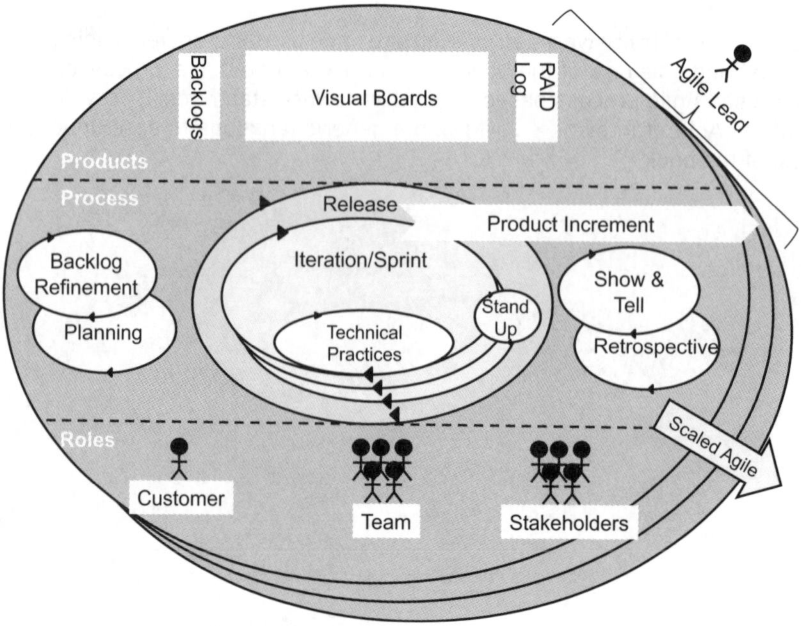

- The customer (see Section 6.1) continually evolves the overall product backlog (see Section 7.1.3) with help from the team (see Section 6.2) and the stakeholders (see Section 6.4).

- The team deliver product increments (see Section 10.3) from iteration/sprints; possibly within releases, and governed in a 'project' or 'BAU' delivery style (see Section 2.4).

- The team perform planning at different levels (release and/or iteration/sprint) and if Agile is scaled, possibly across projects and/or Agile release trains (a 'SAFe' term, see Section 14.8).

- The team create releases, backlogs and/or iteration/sprint backlogs (see Section 7.1.3).

- Delivery is technically enabled using Agile technical practices (see Section 8.10).

- Stand-ups (see Section 8.9) are performed on a daily basis within an iteration/sprint or possibly less regularly for releases.

- Everyone can monitor the status of what is happening within the iteration/sprint or release using visual boards (see Section 8.7).

- Risks, issues, assumptions and dependencies are added to and monitored on the RAID log (see Section 8.7.4).

- Once the product increment is delivered from the iteration/sprint and/or release the team and customer will 'show and tell' (see Section 8.4) the stakeholders about the product delivered. This gives them the opportunity to comment on the current product and highlight suitability and the next planning period (iteration/sprint or release). Any risks and so on will be added to the RAID log.

- The team will perform a retrospective (see Section 8.5) to discuss what went well, what didn't go well and what to do differently next time.

- The Agile lead (see Section 6.3) is responsible for facilitating and enabling the Agile process and for coaching the team to be the best they can be.

- Agile may be scaled up from the iteration/sprint and release level across many teams. This may be delivered in a combination of projects and/or in a BAU style (see Section 2.4).

5.1 AGILE OPERATING MODEL

There is no single Agile framework that provides everything that a business requires to deliver and govern information technology products. Each framework has something to offer; however, they typically need to be integrated with each other (e.g. architectural frameworks) to provide an overall 'Agile operating model' (AOM) for the business.

There is no 'one size fits all' integrated Agile solution; rather the solution is dependent on the business within which Agile is being implemented. However, to aid understanding, Figure 5.2 gives a purposefully simple representation of what may be suitable in some situations.

Figure 5.2 is obviously an over-simplification as the actual frameworks overlap and do not just operate within the strict boundaries described above. To give a brief overview:

Figure 5.2 Agile operating model

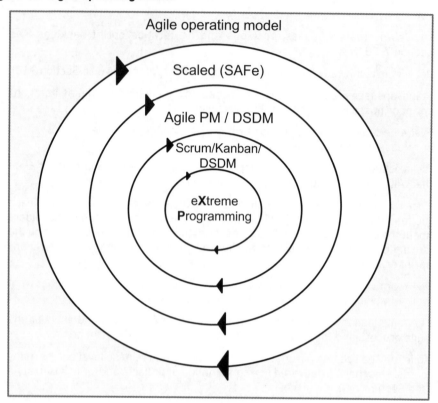

- eXtreme Programming (see Section 14.1) is generally focused on the more technical (and team) aspects of software engineering.

- Scrum (see Section 14.2), Kanban (see Section 14.5) or DSDM (see Section 14.3) are more focused on the team and product delivery.

- Agile PM (see Section 14.4) or DSDM (see Section 14.3) can be used if Agile project governance is required (see Section 2.4).

- If the Agile delivery involves many teams, then a scaled Agile framework like SAFe (see Section 14.8) may be suitable.

- All these are wrapped within the Agile values and principles described in the Agile Manifesto (see Section 1.2).

When the frameworks are integrated and work together in this way, they create the Agile operating model. The AOM can then integrate with other frameworks (like those in Figure 5.3) to create an overall business (or department) operating model (BOM).

Figure 5.3 Agile business operating model

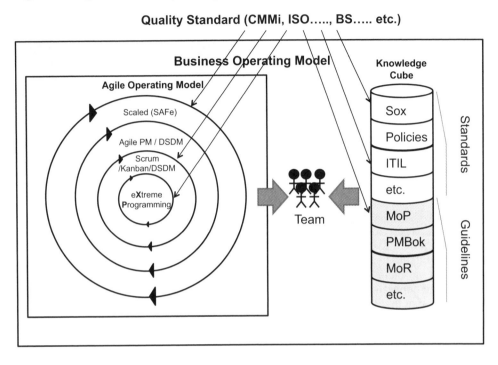

To give an overview of Figure 5.3 Agile business operating model:

- The AOM is part of the BOM.

- A 'knowledge cube' is described within the BOM – this is a repository of everything that the organisation or department needs to run effectively.

- Typically there will be standards and guidelines in the knowledge cube: a standard is something that is mandatory and audited, whereas a guideline is something that can be inspected and adapted by the team.

- The key is to keep the AOM as simple as possible so teams can understand it easily and therefore use it.

- If a quality assurance approach is to be implemented in the organisation (e.g. CMMi (n.d.) or an ISO standard), then this will reference the BOM (and therefore the AOM and knowledge cube) that describes how compliance is being achieved.

6 COMMON AGILE ROLES

Each Agile framework (see Chapter 14) has its own view on the different roles in an Agile delivery, with their own names and structure. The roles that are discussed in this chapter occur generically across the majority of Agile frameworks focused on the team level; there are other roles, such as Agile project manager, that would typically be applied when delivering Agile projects (see Section 14.4) or scaling Agile (see Section 14.8), but will not be covered here.

There are generally four key roles in an Agile delivery: the customer, the Agile lead, the Agile team itself and stakeholders. Figure 6.1 highlights the typical skills that will be required in an Agile team; however, an Agile approach aims for team members to be 'specialised generalists' (see Section 6.2.2) rather than just having one skill. The dotted lines represent that there may be many other stakeholders and many other supporting skills that contribute to the team but may not be part of the core team (e.g. architect skills).

Figure 6.1 Generic Agile roles

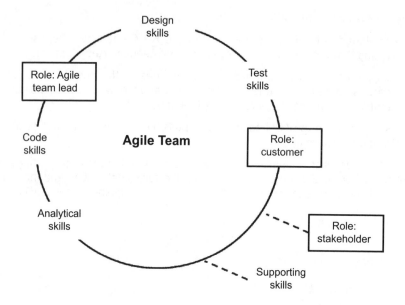

In the following sections, we will look at the four roles in more detail.

6.1 THE CUSTOMER

'Customer' in an Agile context means the person who makes the decisions about what will be done in what order, and the term normally refers to the owner of the product being built. The customer has to be able to answer the question 'Why are we doing this?' – essentially they are responsible for the 'vision' of the product.

The customer also

- defines what stories are to be delivered;
- decides the order of the stories on the backlog;
- signs off stories as 'done' (see Section 10.2) at the end of each iteration/sprint or release.

A good and regularly used mnemonic for remembering the key criteria of a 'good customer' is 'DARK(a)', which stands for...

D is for Desire A customer should want to be involved in and excited about the product being delivered.

A is for Authority The customer should have the authority to make decisions and enforce them. It must be clear to the customer, team and stakeholders what decisions the customer can and cannot make. For example, the customer working with a team may be part of a larger project of multiple teams and therefore they would not have the authority to make decisions concerning the larger project. For the decisions the customer cannot make it must be clear who can make those decisions and what the turnaround time will be; this is key to enabling planning.

R is for Responsibility The customer is (amongst other things) responsible for defining what the team will deliver and in which order.

K is for Knowledgeable This does not mean that the customer has to be the font of all knowledge but it does mean that they must know where to find the information in a timely manner.

A is for Availability When working in small, focused cycles, it is vital that any decisions are made in the same timely manner and any questions are answered as quickly as possible. This cannot happen if the customer is absent. This does not necessarily mean that the customer needs to be co-located and available 24/7. However, the role is responsible for the day-to-day communication channels between the team and the business.

The role and responsibilities of the customer are also covered in the following Agile Manifesto statements and principles.

6.1.1 Customer collaboration over contract negotiation

There is value in defining a contract in an Agile delivery; however, the contract is more about stating clearly the collaboration between the customer and the team, rather than focusing on up-front analysis and design. The contract will identify the customer, their agreed level of authority, who will make any decisions they cannot make, and in what timescale these decisions will need to be made.

6.1.2 Our highest priority is to satisfy the customer through early and continuous delivery of valuable software

An Agile delivery focuses on delivering value to the customer as early as possible and in a continuous manner. To enable this, the customer needs to define the stories that they require, together with the value associated with those stories and the order in which they want them delivered. The customer is responsible for creating stories in collaboration with stakeholders and the team.

Arguably the key word in this manifesto principle is 'valuable'. If for some reason the team (for example) have added stories to the backlog on their own and the customer does not understand the stories, collaboration becomes difficult and risk is introduced. Therefore it is essential that the way the stories are described makes sense to the customer and uses non-technical language and as little jargon as possible.

6.1.3 Welcome changing requirements, even late in development. Agile processes harness change for the customer's competitive advantage

Agile designs emerge as the product is being developed (see Section 9.2). This means that any changed or new requirement that gives the customer added capability to deliver competitive advantage quickly and continuously can be added into the delivery based on comparative business value.

In a time-boxed delivery, if the stories to be delivered change right at the end of the project or release, then neither Waterfall nor Agile will save the project. However, in Agile this scenario is extremely rare because the team delivers stories continuously in short iterations/sprints, and continually interacts with all stakeholders, demonstrating to them the working software that has been developed. Therefore it will be extremely unusual that fundamental requirement changes occur right at the end of a release or project.

6.1.4 Business people and developers must work together daily throughout the project

To enable continuous delivery of valuable product, business people (i.e. stakeholders and customers) and the team must work together throughout the project. If this does not happen, the product that is developed is highly unlikely to be suitable for the customer.

6.1.5 The most efficient and effective method of conveying information to and within a development team is face-to-face conversation

The role of the customer in the team is to enable accurate communication and fast feedback cycles. To effectively convey information, the customer and team must have the ability to communicate face-to-face, whether that is physically or virtually (see Section 8.2).

6.2 THE TEAM

Agile teams are typically responsible for:

- Deciding how to do the work. This involves refining stories with the customer and then (typically) dividing them into tasks.

- Defining how long the work will take. With the detailed task breakdown, the team will be able to provide a more accurate estimate of the effort needed to complete each task. Typically, tasks will be broken down to be completed in less than 10 hours (2 days) of effort.

- Deciding who does the work. During the daily stand-up meeting (see Section 8.3), the team will have an opportunity to examine the progress achieved and decide how to best organise themselves to deliver maximum value to the customer.

- Delivering the product.

As we've seen in Section 6.1 the customer is responsible for defining what stories will be developed in what order, relying on support from the team. At iteration/sprint planning the team will then subdivide these stories into tasks, decide who will deliver the tasks and how long (typically in hours) delivery will take. Very experienced teams may not plan at task level as their level of skill and experience enables them to deliver effectively without that level of planning. However, it is generally a mistake to not go down to the task level in planning, as this is a very common cause of sprint/iteration goals being missed.

6.2.1 Specialised generalists

Agile teams should consist of members who are 'specialised generalists'. A specialised generalist is someone who does have a specialist skill (like testing skill) as well as a general understanding of what everyone else in the team does. For example, in a football team each member would have a specialist skill (e.g. goalkeeper, centre forward), but they would also have general skills such as the ability to tackle, kick the ball and so on.

Having a team made up of only specialists can make communication and therefore collaboration and teamwork very difficult as the understanding of what everyone else in the team is doing can be missing. Typical specialist skills that can be found in an Agile team are:

- architectural skill;
- analytical skill;
- design skill;
- coding skill;
- testing skill;
- business knowledge.

6.2.2 Self-organising teams

Agile teams are generally set up as self-organising teams, meaning they have the authority to decide how work gets done, who does it and how long it should take. This does not mean that they have carte blanche to do whatever they like. Teams will typically be operating within a structure of high-level standards and guidelines that ensure consistency across a programme, project or organisation. Part of the skill of the Agile lead (see Section 6.3) is to decide where to put these constraints for the good of the overall organisation and the good of the team, without adversely affecting self-organisation.

Most self-organising teams, for example, would not have the authority to choose who is on the team, what business problem they are expected to help solve, or even what budget they have. Even from a technical perspective, most teams would not have a free choice to use any architecture or toolset they think was appropriate as these limits are often imposed by external enterprise or system architects.

Being part of a self-organising team allows team members to learn and adjust constantly as they develop the product, which in turn leads to better architectures, requirements and designs. This principle is based on the understanding that software development is knowledge-based work, and a knowledge worker is somebody who knows more about their job than their boss (Drucker, 2001).

Table 6.1 shows examples of behaviours from self-organising teams and teams that are managed by command and control.

Table 6.1 Typical differences between team types

Command-and-control teams	Self-organised teams
Take directions	Take initiative
Seek individual reward	Focus on team contributions
Focus on low-level objectives	Concentrate on solutions
Compete	Cooperate
Comply with processes regardless of outcome	Continually look for better ways of working
React to emergencies	Take steps to prevent emergencies

Other reasons why self-organising teams tend towards better performance for software development work (30–50% or more (Orsburn, 1990)) are:

- **Fast decision making** – many decisions don't need to go up the management chain.

- **Increased motivation** – due to a greater sense of autonomy.

- **Increased brain power** – instead of a single manager working on a problem, there is the potential to apply the brain power of the entire team.

- **Increased levels of initiative and continuous improvement** – to the point where team members start to consider the goals of the team to be more important than their own personal goals.

6.2.3 Feature teams

An Agile feature team concentrates on producing ordered stories, refined as value-add features in the value sequence that the customer requires (see Figure 6.2). It contains whatever skills are required to deliver the stories to the customer and is a key driver in the reduction of 'waste' in the value chain (see Chapter 13).

Figure 6.2 The Agile feature team

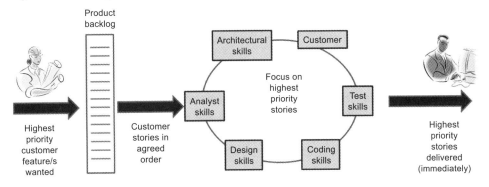

Agile teams are usually structured as feature teams as it enables delivery of features (described as stories) from the backlog in vertical slices (see Section 13.2). This allows for regular delivery of value-add features to the customer.

6.2.4 Component teams

Sometimes – in particular when Agile is scaled across large complex deliveries – it is not realistic for all teams to be feature teams as it may only be possible to deliver features to the customer once a number of components have been delivered and integrated. This is when component teams are required. Component teams are responsible for producing components that can be combined with other components from other teams and integrated together into a feature.

So for example, the production of a mobile phone operating system would require many Agile teams, some of them component teams, as it would be very difficult for a single team to deliver features that a phone user would understand within weeks or months.

6.2.5 Core and support teams

In large and complex deliveries, it is quite typical to find core teams that are focused on delivering across the value chain, as well as some support teams (e.g. possibly architecture support or user interface support). A typical size of a core team is somewhere between three and nine people, not including the customer, the Agile lead or support people.

Support teams exist specifically to support and enable the core teams to do things right first time; not to 'police' the core teams and tell them when they have done something wrong at a delivery gateway.

6.3 THE AGILE LEAD

The role of an Agile lead is a multifaceted one. It is named and described differently in different Agile frameworks, but the Agile lead's main responsibility across all frameworks is to enable their team to self-organise and continually improve. Some Agile frameworks see the Agile lead role as a change agent; others describe the role to include more team leadership responsibilities in addition to the change agent capabilities.

An Agile lead should have the following characteristics:

- experience and maturity to understand that the focus in Agile is on the individuals and the effective face-to-face interactions between those individuals;
- the ability to create a no-blame culture where people are not afraid to try new things, and an understanding that everyone (including themselves) makes mistakes, and that mistakes are acceptable as long as learning occurs;
- experience in and knowledge of Agile;
- experience in transformation.

The Agile lead should also have an appreciation of the aspects detailed in the following subsections.

6.3.1 Agile lead as 'servant-leader'

The term 'servant-leader' was termed in 1970 in an essay by Robert K. Greenleaf:

> The Servant-Leader is servant first... It begins with the natural feeling that one wants to serve, to serve first. Then conscious choice brings one to aspire to lead. That person is sharply different from one who is leader first; perhaps because of the need to assuage an unusual power drive or to acquire material possessions.

(Greenleaf, 1970)

An Agile lead should be a servant-leader who gains the credibility in their team by being a servant to the team's needs and wants. They will not command and control the team; instead they will facilitate and enable the team to self-organise.

In contrast, a team lead who operates in a 'command and control' style will typically pass a plan to the team that details how they should do things (tasks) and how long they have to do those things; they will then control the team to achieve the plan. If the team fails, which is likely because they will not buy into a plan they had little or no input to, the team will probably blame the team lead for the failure citing excuses such as 'we knew the plan was wrong'. The team will also not self-organise as they have no motivation for doing so and they won't feel safe to do so.

6.3.2 Removing impediments

An Agile lead is also responsible for supporting the team in identifying and finding ways of removing anything that blocks a task from being executed or a feature from being delivered. Impediments might include:

- management command and control behaviours;
- little support from management for Agile way of working;
- implementing Agile within a Waterfall management environment;
- ineffective transformation – nothing ever changes;
- technology that blocks Agile capability;
- lack of empowerment;
- lack of ability to self-organise;
- organisation not structured to enable agility.

Sometimes impediments can also simply be interruptions that the team may experience, such as being continuously asked to 'just do this or that'. All interruptions create noise that can impede the team, and therefore hinder delivery. The Agile lead should remove as much noise from the team as possible.

6.3.3 Workshop facilitator

Many Agile frameworks describe activities that are most effectively delivered as workshops, for example 'show and tells' (see Section 8.4). All of these activities and any other ad-hoc workshops need to be structured and facilitated, and it is common for Agile leads to take on this role.

As a facilitator should, if possible, be independent from the people who attend the workshop, it may be a good idea for the lead from team A to facilitate workshops for team B and vice versa.

6.3.4 Process facilitator

Another responsibility of Agile leads is to help the organisation, programme, project or team to define an Agile operating model (see Section 5.1). So for example, Agile leads need to make sure the team's definition of 'done' or process policies are being met (see Section 10.2.1), that work in progress limits are being adhered to, that all Agile activities are respected, and that stories are refined to the appropriate size.

Agile leads should also guide their team to identify areas of their processes that they can improve and should introduce process improvements by facilitating the self-organising team rather than by imposing them.

6.3.5 Coach/trainer

Agile leads should pass on their knowledge of Agile principles, processes and practices to their team through coaching and training. Transformation starts with visualisation – if the group to be transformed cannot visualise why they should transform, they won't!

Agile leads will often champion the implementation of new technical practices. Agile adoption does not always mandate the need for new technical practices and tools, but they are often good enablers for a team to become more Agile. This means that Agile leads need to have a good understanding of technical practices; eXtreme Programming (see Section 14.1) is a good place to start the journey to this level of understanding.

Implementation of new practices needs to be done with the buy-in of the team, following the principles of self-organisation. If new practices are imposed upon the team by the Agile lead without the team buying in to them, they are likely to fail.

6.4 THE STAKEHOLDERS

The term stakeholder refers to all the people and organisations that have a real or perceived 'stake' in the project or its outcomes. PRINCE2 defines a stakeholder as:

> Parties with an interest in the execution and outcome of a project. They would include business streams affected by or dependent on the outcome.

(PRINCE2, 2011)

The *PMBOK® Guide* (*A Guide to the Project Management Body of Knowledge*) (PMI, 2013) describes a stakeholder as a person or organisation that:

* is actively involved in the project;
* has interests that may be positively or negatively affected by the performance or completion of the project;
* may exert influence over the project, its deliverables or its team members.

Another definition may be: 'Any person or group who can help us, or hinder.'

Identifying and effectively managing stakeholders is key to any delivery's success, as they can champion a project and help drive success, or be very effective saboteurs. Powerful stakeholders are much more likely to sabotage a project if they don't feel engaged.

Many projects fail to involve one or more critically important stakeholders during project definition and planning. The resulting problems are easily predictable: requirements conflicts and rework, at a minimum; and sometimes more dire consequences, including lawsuits or hefty fines.

(Verzuh, 2008)

The role of the stakeholder in an Agile delivery is to ensure that the interests of the group they are part of are represented. In the majority of Agile frameworks the customer defines what the team will do in what order by interacting with the stakeholders. However, direct interaction between the team and the stakeholders is also encouraged as it enables the team to ascertain key information they need to deliver an effective product.

6.4.1 Identifying stakeholders

There are a number of techniques to identify effective stakeholders:

- Organisation charts and directories. Perhaps the first place to look for stakeholders is the company organisation chart or directory.

- Stakeholder lists. Creating a generic list of all stakeholders that may be involved in any product delivery is a good starting point to help new product deliveries identify potential stakeholders.

- Previous projects. Documentation from previous projects and talking to project teams can help to identify stakeholders that may have to be involved in a particular project type.

- Brainstorming and capturing every name, organisation or type of stakeholder that the participants in a workshop can think of is another great way of identifying stakeholders.

6.4.2 Stakeholder analysis

Once stakeholders have been identified, the next stage is to complete a stakeholder analysis. Different methodologies suggest different ways of analysing stakeholders, some complex and some very simple. The aim is to prioritise stakeholders in order of importance. A common approach is to map the interest and power or influence of each stakeholder group on a quadrant (Bryson, 2013; Figure 6.3).

- **High power/high interest** – these are key players and should be involved in governance and decision making. It is important to keep them engaged and to consult them regularly.

- **High power/low interest** – these should be consulted on their interest area with a view to increasing their level of interest. The aim is to move them into the high power/high interest quadrant. The danger with these stakeholders is that they perform 'seagull management' – they fly into the delivery intermittently, dump on everything, and then fly out again.

Figure 6.3 Stakeholder power/interest mapping grid

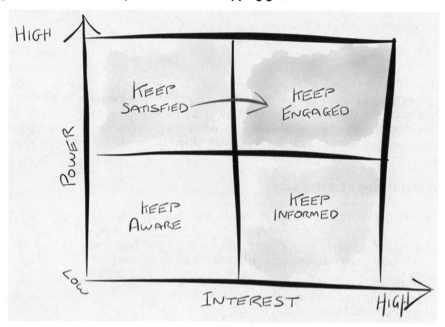

- **High interest/low power** – stakeholders in this group can be engaged by involving them in low-risk areas, keeping them informed and consulting on interest area. In fact the more creative and unexpected stories often come from the stakeholders in this bottom-right quadrant as this group are naturally interested in the product and often form an evangelist community of early adopters. The key with this community is to keep them interested and offer them early access to new stories (alpha community, focus groups, etc.).

- **Low interest/low power** – this group needs to be kept aware of what is going on via general communications: newsletters, websites, mailshots and so on.

Completing a power/interest grid will help to develop a communication plan that is aligned to each stakeholder's focus and concerns.

7 COMMON AGILE TECHNIQUES

7.1 STORIES AND BACKLOG REFINEMENT

Stories define what is required from the team by the customer and stakeholders (see Chapter 5). A story is not a detailed specification of a requirement; rather, it is a token or reminder for the team that a feature (or anything else that is value-add – for example, a story driving the creation of a security standard) needs to be delivered.

Stories should include:

- **WHO** wants a feature. It is good practice to write the 'Who' statement in the stories from the perspective of an 'Agile persona'. An Agile persona is any person or group (a 'user') who will interact with the features being created. The reason that stories are written from the perspective of an Agile persona is that it facilitates creation of stories that make sense to stakeholders and the customer.
- **WHAT** feature they want.
- **WHY** they want the feature. This may be tied into a business case if one exists.
- **ACCEPTANCE CRITERIA.** This is normally a list of questions, scenarios or examples that enable the customer to sign off the story as 'done' (see below for more information and Section 10.2.1 for more information about 'done').

Stories usually comprise a story card (a physical or virtual piece of card that describes the information above; see Figure 7.1), any conversation(s) between the customer and team (that may be added to the card) and, after the feature has been delivered, confirmation from the customer that the delivery meets acceptance criteria. A typically used format and syntax for stories is:

- **As a** (the 'who') ...
- **I want** (the 'what') ...
- **So that** (the 'why') ...
- **Acceptance criteria**

> **Box 7.1 An example of story writing**
>
> This is an example of how a story might be written, relating to an Agile persona: 'Mike – the Business Development Manager'.

As a – Business Development Manager

I want – the ability to identify all people who have registered or re-registered on our system in the last 3 months

So that – I can send focused marketing material to those people

Acceptance criteria –

- Can I identify all people who have registered or re-registered in the last 3 months from today's date?
- Can I identify basic demographics (name, age, email address) relating to those people?
- Is it clear what the core preferences, via site usage, of those people are?
- Do I know how many times these people have logged on in the last 3 months?
- Do I know how much those people have spent with us each month?
- Do I know what products these people have ordered each month?
- Am I prevented from seeing people who registered or re-registered outside the 3 month timeline? (this is an example of a 'negative' acceptance criteria written as a 'positive' question).

Figure 7.1 Story cards

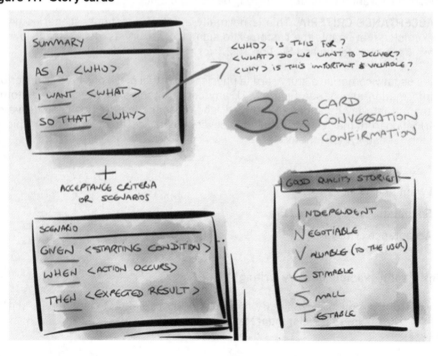

Stories can be of any size, and they tend to be refined as the product is developed, down from very large size (known as 'coarse-grained stories'), which could be months of effort in size to very small (known as 'fine-grained stories'), which are typically 1–5 days' effort in size.

Stories are placed in a backlog, which is essentially a 'to-do' list where stories are arranged in an agreed delivery sequence. Stories in a backlog are continually refined throughout the whole lifetime of the product. This lifetime could be anything from a couple of months (e.g. a marketing campaign) to many decades (e.g. a banking system). The customer and the team refine stories on an ongoing basis throughout the whole lifetime of the product. It is expected that stories will change and be refined, because the team are working in an environment of high variability (see Section 2.2).

> A common mistake made by teams is that they write technical stories that do not make sense to the customer. This inhibits agility as the customer cannot provide a priority/sequence in which to deliver the feature as they do not understand the story; and it also inhibits collaboration between the team, customer and stakeholders.

A good way to understand the characteristics of good stories is the acronym 'INVEST'. It stands for:

Independent Stories should be deliverable independently of each other. This is generally feasible at the coarse-grained level but can become more difficult as stories become more fine-grained. Creating independent stories also enables the team and customer to inject small stories into the backlog that can be delivered in timescales aligned to iterations/sprints ('Feature Injection'; Matts, 2013).

Negotiable A story is not a detailed specification of requirements; rather it is something that will be refined over time, and is negotiable up until the point that the story is planned within a sprint.

Valuable It is essential that the value of a story is understood by the customer. Only if the customer can identify the value of a story can it be ordered within the backlog. This means a common, non-jargon-laden language for all stories is fundamentally important.

Estimable The story is the unit against which plans and estimates are created. Stories must be understood by the team as they are responsible for creating estimates. Therefore it is essential that the team is involved in the refinement of stories, in cooperation with the customer and stakeholders. Only then will the team have a solid understanding of the story and be able to create realistic and achievable estimates.

Small enough A common mistake when writing a story is to provide too much information too soon. Generally, it is recommended that stories are refined to the 1 to 5 days' effort size just before the next iteration/sprint is planned.

Testable Stories must include testable acceptance criteria in order to achieve 'done' status (see Section 10.2.1). While acceptance criteria are not detailed tests (see Section 7.1.2), they will be driving what the tests will be.

7.1.1 Planning pyramid

As mentioned above, it is good practice to keep stories independent of each other, and to have as few parent–child levels as possible. However, when delivering large, complex projects, there may be dependencies between stories, and a feature breakdown structure of parent–child stories may be required; this is known as a 'planning pyramid' (see Figure 7.2).

Figure 7.2 Planning pyramid

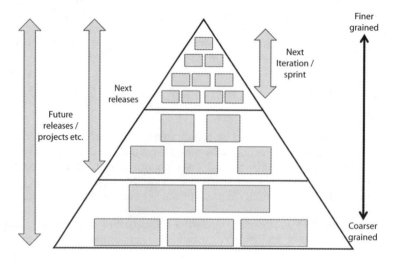

A planning pyramid contains both coarse-grained and fine-grained stories; the coarse-grained stories are being refined to be fine-grained stories as delivery progresses. If planning is required over a longer timescale than just the next sprint, stories will only be refined to the most coarse-grained level that enables this (see Section 7.2). When delivering a product that requires a delivery estimate, a simple end-to-end prototype would typically be created that gives a high-level description of the product to be delivered. This enables very high level planning and estimation, and the creation of a predicted end-date for the delivery. At all times, the core point to remember is that it is highly likely the product will change during the development cycle.

7.1.2 Scenario-based acceptance criteria

Previously, we described an example of how a story could be written from the perspective of an Agile persona, including a number of acceptance criteria. This style of writing acceptance criteria is normally associated with an Agile practice called 'Test Driven Development' (TDD – see Section 7.4).

In 2004 Dan North (North, 2006) suggested a thought experiment called 'BDD' (Behaviour Driven Development – see Section 7.4) to complement TDD. Behaviour Driven Development is concerned with the behaviour of the system, which means that the acceptance criteria in BDD are usually expressed as scenarios. Here is a simple example of how to write acceptance criteria in BDD:

As a – generic bank customer

I want – the ability to withdraw cash from an ATM

So that – I don't have to visit the branch continually to draw money

Acceptance criteria:

Scenario One: the bank account is in credit

Given

– the customer requires to draw cash from the ATM

When

– the customer enters their card to the machine

– and the bank account is in credit

Then

– debit bank account

– and update transaction statement

– and return card

– and dispense cash

Scenario Two: the bank account has hit overdraft limit

Given

– the customer requires to draw cash from the ATM

When

– the customer enters their card to the machine

– and the bank account has hit overdraft limit

Then

– return card

– and display message 'overdraft limit reached'

– and offer customer other services

BDD is generally implemented on coarse-grained stories more suited to scenario-based acceptance criteria, while TDD is implemented on fine-grained stories where a question-driven approach is more suitable.

7.1.3 Backlog refinement and 'spike' stories

Stories are continually refined within the backlog throughout the whole lifetime of the product, which could be a couple of months (e.g. a marketing campaign), or could possibly be many decades (e.g. banking system).

This means that stories will continue to evolve from inception of the product through to decommissioning the backlog. In particular in complicated, complex or anarchic environments it is fundamental that stories evolve in line with the changing environment. This is unnecessarily difficult to do if the stories have too much detail, and/or are created too early within the delivery. Instead, stories should be refined on a 'just-in-time' basis for the next sprint (this idea aligns to a concept in Lean called 'last responsible moment' (see Section 9.2)).

A common mistake is that teams write and refine all or many of the stories that may be required before actually developing anything. This often happens when a team is being asked to give an estimate for the whole product delivery (see Section 7.2 for guidance on Agile estimating); however, if a team do this they are basically just doing a Waterfall delivery, having performed an 'analysis' stage by defining and refining all stories up front. In Agile deliveries, stories are refined continually on a 'just in time' basis.

Agile teams sometimes quote YAGNI as a good acronym to keep in mind when thinking about whether a feature should be added to a product or not. YAGNI stands for 'You Ain't Gonna Need It' and can be applied when deciding whether stories should be added to the backlog. For example, if the product is only going to be live for a short period of time, then the technical quality of the product may not need to be particularly robust.

A spike story (a term originally from eXtreme Programming (see Section 14.1)) is a story that drives technical or functional research effort or investigative work. Creating a spike story is different to refining stories in the backlog; backlog refinement is an ongoing process of analysis and design; spiking, on the other hand, is initiating a story-driven activity to investigate something specific.

7.1.4 Prioritisation (with 'MSCW')

Prioritisation is key to all Agile frameworks because they all largely implement time-boxing (see Section 2.4.2.1). A time-box is a boxed period of time (e.g. a project, release or sprint/iteration) in which something will be delivered in a prioritised sequence.

There is a subtle difference between 'ordering' and 'prioritising' that is timescale-related. A backlog is a 'to-do' list of items, normally stories, which will be delivered in an agreed order throughout the lifetime of the product – from inception to decommissioning. Once some of the stories are planned into a project or release or iteration/sprint time-box, then prioritisation can be used to arrange them in a sequence within the time-box.

MSCW (pronounced MoSCoW) is a prioritisation technique that is the intellectual property of the DSDM Consortium (see Section 14.3), however, it is free to use and is used by many Agile teams (see Figure 7.3).

Figure 7.3 MSCW prioritisation

The MSCW acronym stands for the following features:

M – must have Sometimes also termed as the MVP (minimum viable product), or the MMFS (minimum marketable feature set). These are the stories that **must** be delivered within a particular time-box. Not delivering these stories and still delivering the product means the solution is non-viable, illegal or pointless.

S – should have A story that is very important within a time-box, and that will cause significant problems to the customer if not delivered, though the customer could still get value from the product if this feature is not in place.

C – could have A story that is very important within a time-box and may cause some problems to the customer if not delivered. However, the customer will still gain value from the product if a 'could have' feature is not in place.

W – won't have this time It can be agreed between a customer and team that a particular story won't be delivered in a particular time-box. This story might be added to a later time-box or removed completely from the backlog.

Once a time-box is finished, all missing stories should be reviewed and the priorities re-evaluated. A particular story may be a 'must have' feature for delivery at the end of a six-month project, but may only be a 'should have' feature for delivery at the end of a three-month release. The same feature may be a 'could have' feature for delivery within the first two-week sprint/iteration time-box.

It is important to understand that MSCW prioritisation is specifically designed for implementation within fixed time frames. If MSCW is implemented on a backlog without a time frame, it is very likely that a customer will define everything within the backlog as a 'must have'.

> The best way to think about MSCW prioritisation is 'Within **this** specific time frame I must have/should have/could have/won't have this feature.'

Another reason why MSCW prioritisation sometimes fails is if stories are defined at a very coarse-grained level. Again this will lead the customer to perceive them all as 'must haves' – for example, an e-commerce website must have a payment method, but there are opportunities to prioritise depending on the type, rigour, security and so on of payment method used.

One way of achieving MSCW prioritisation is to understand that there is more than one way to develop a feature. So the 'must have' story may be a basic implementation of a feature that enables the customer to gain value. Subsequently the 'could have' story can be a much more 'gold plated' version of the feature that the customer would ideally like. For example, the customer could require a date management service that manages all worldwide date formats, however, they must have a service that manages UK date format next month.

7.2 AGILE ESTIMATION

Agile estimates are forecasts of how many stories can be delivered within any time period (for example, in a project or a release iteration/sprint).

Story size and a team's capacity to deliver stories (or 'velocity' – see below) are estimated in either 'ideal days' or 'story points'. Story points and ideal days are specifically associated with 'top-down' estimation and planning (see Section 7.3.1; Figure 7.4).

It is important to remember that any estimates and plans in an Agile delivery tend to be made in uncertain and possibly volatile environments and therefore can only ever be baseline forecasts.

7.2.1 Ideal days

Ideal days are what project management frameworks call 'productive time'; in essence the time that is allocated to deliver planned items (mainly stories) from the backlog. Time that is allocated to do other things such as answering telephone calls or emails, attending meetings and so on is often termed 'non-productive time' (although realistically it is not non-productive as this work and the associated time is also essential).

Figure 7.4 Agile estimation with story points

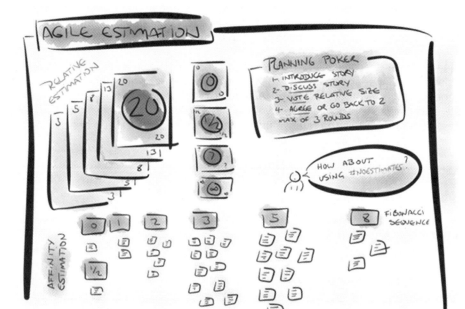

Many Agile teams tend to avoid estimates based on ideal days because once time is associated with coarse-grained stories teams may add contingency and 'Parkinson's law' ('work expands to fit time available'; Oxford Dictionary, 2014) may apply. Estimates based on time also carry the risk of too much up-front analysis and design being performed to ensure that the time-based estimate is 'accurate'. Instead, many Agile teams use story points to create estimates because they are not directly related to time, meaning the issues described above are removed.

7.2.2 Story points and planning poker

Story points provide a way of relatively estimating story sizes, leading to a plan of how many stories can be delivered within a given time-box (for example, a project or release – see Section 7.3). Story points estimate the relative effort required to develop a particular story. As Mike Cohn, the originator of the concept of story points, says on one of his blogs, 'Story points are not about the complexity of developing a feature; they are about the effort required to develop a feature' (Cohn, n.d.).

Story points provide relative size estimates for stories. People use relative sizing all the time in their day-to-day lives: for example, they talk about one building being large and another building being small; or about one car being 'small-medium' and another car being 'medium-large'. Any new story can be relatively sized against the other stories already sized in the backlog.

Story points are generally determined by a team within a 'planning poker' workshop (Grenning, 2002), where they agree the relative effort (story points) required to deliver stories to 'done' status (see Section 10.2) on a scale from 0 to 100.

Planning poker typically uses a relative sizing based partly on a Fibonacci sequence as this describes fine- and coarse-grained differences between numbers. This numbering sequence aligns with the different relative sizes of stories. The relative differences between stories that are near to delivery will be fine-grained (because the stories have been refined), whereas the relative differences between stories that are further away from delivery will be coarse-grained.

Typical story-point sizes in planning poker are:

- The story is at 'done' status = 0
- Fine-grained sizings = ½ (xxs), 1 (xs), 2 (s), 3 (sm), 5 (m), 8 (ml), 13 (l) – the Fibonacci sequence
- Coarse-grained sizings = 20 (xl), 40 (xxl), 100 (xxxl)
- Not enough knowledge to estimate this story = ?
- The story is so big it's impossible to estimate or that the team do not have the capability to deliver the story at all = ∞ (infinity)

Using an architectural analogy: if a team identified the story 'Building a large shed' as requiring the least effort, they would size this story at (s) small (or '2' in the Fibonacci sequence). Other stories can now be sized relatively to this story. So, for example, the story 'Building a simple bedsit' may be relatively sized as (sm) 'small-medium' effort (5 in the Fibonacci sequence). This process continues until enough stories have been sized to enable planning.

7.3 AGILE PLANNING

Plans in an Agile delivery are specifically created to enable change. There are differing levels of plans in Agile frameworks, including portfolio, programme, project, release and iteration/sprint plans. This section will concentrate on release and iteration/sprint plans as these are fairly common across all Agile frameworks.

Many of the ideas that have become standard in relation to Agile estimating and planning are described in the book of the same name from Mike Cohn (2005).

7.3.1 Top-down and bottom-up planning

7.3.1.1 Top-down planning

Where variability is likely to be experienced it is highly risky to try and define a detailed plan, as there will be a significant overhead if it needs to be changed. Top-down plans (created by the team) are purposely quick and inexact and are especially suited to variable environments where things are likely to change.

Top-down planning is specifically associated with creating estimates for longer time frames, such as a release. When planning a release the accuracy of estimates will improve continually based on lessons learned throughout the life of the project (see Section 2.5).

Top-down planning can be performed with either 'story points' or 'ideal days' (see previous sections). Top-down planning is normally based on previous experience or existing reliable data.

An example could be assessing how long it will take to travel somewhere. If the journey has been done a few times before then top-down planning would use that previous experience and assume that the next time the journey will take an average of what it has taken previously.

7.3.1.2 Bottom-up planning

When a more detailed estimate is required, for example when committing to deliver in short iteration/sprint timescales of a few weeks, a bottom-up planning approach may be used and possibly calibrated with a top-down estimate.

In bottom-up planning, teams typically know which stories are likely to be delivered in the iteration/sprint based on top-down planning. The team then identify what capacity they have to deliver these stories; this is normally expressed as 'total available hours' within an iteration/sprint. The team then plan all the tasks that are required to get the stories to 'done' status, and estimate the hours needed to deliver the planned tasks; this is normally expressed as 'total required hours' in this iteration/sprint.

The 'total required hours' are then compared against the 'total available hours'. If the figures differ, the team remove tasks until the required hours match the available hours. This may mean removing, replacing, adding or splitting some stories from the original top-down forecast.

7.3.2 Release planning and velocity

A release backlog is a subset of the overall backlog that relates to the stories that are forecast to be 'done' in a particular release. Release backlogs are created in a release planning activity at which the whole team, customer and possibly other stakeholders will be present.

To forecast the number of stories that can be done within a particular release backlog, teams must be able to estimate the size of stories using the same unit that they use to size story capacity within the release (ideal days or story points – see Section 7.2).

Once the team have estimated the relative size of the stories in the overall backlog, they then need to size the iterations/sprints within the release using the same unit (e.g. story points). To estimate how many story points can be achieved within an iteration/sprint, teams look to past historical evidence of how many story points they have actually achieved in previous sprints. This is called a 'velocity', i.e. the average number of story points that a team have been able to deliver across the last 1 to 5 iterations/sprints.

Once the team understand their velocity and the size of the stories in the backlog in the same unit (e.g. story points), they can plan the stories into the iterations/sprints in a release. Once all iterations/sprints in a release have stories assigned to them, a forecast plan of how many stories from the backlog can be achieved within a release can be created. At this point the release goal is defined. This is normally a subset of the stories planned into the release to give some slack for unforeseen circumstances.

If a release goal either becomes inaccurate (i.e. it does not deliver what the business now wants) or untenable (i.e. the forecasts were significantly wrong), release planning needs to be re-initiated and a new release goal agreed. This process is very similar at portfolio, programme and project levels.

It is important to keep in mind that release plans are baseline plans, and that they are likely to change as delivery progresses. A significant part of the organisational change to the Agile mindset (see Section 2.1) is therefore to ensure that stakeholders understand that release plans are designed to change, rather than being commitment plans (this is why they are top-down plans. If stakeholders force any plan at a level above the iteration/sprint plan to be a commitment plan, it will typically only achieve the delivery of the wrong product, because it does not allow for the plan to respond to changing business needs.

7.3.3 Iteration/sprint planning

Iteration/sprint planning is usually performed in two parts, often named 'Planning part 1' and 'Planning part 2'.

7.3.3.1 Iteration/sprint planning part 1

Sprint planning part 1 is an example of top-down planning (see above), and is performed in the same way as release planning – i.e. the team plan the number of stories to be delivered within an iteration/sprint based on story-point size and velocity.

7.3.3.2 Iteration/sprint planning part 2

Sprint planning part 2 is an example of bottom-up planning (see Section 7.3.1.2). When the forecast number of stories that can be delivered from top-down and bottom-up estimates match, this is likely to be a robust estimate that the team are able to commit to. If the figures do not match then the team will need to ascertain the reasons for the discrepancy to the point where they believe they have arrived at a robust estimate for the iteration/sprint.

7.4 AGILE TESTING

A core principle of Agile quality control is that testing (validation) is integrated throughout the entire lifecycle. All types of testing need to be implemented early and continuously and should never be left to the end of a release period, as significant defects found at that point can seriously derail delivery or quality of the product.

Many Agile frameworks align to the concepts described in the book *Agile Testing* by Lisa Crispin and Janet Gregory (Crispin and Gregory, 2009) in their approach to quality control and testing. The book presents an evolution of the 'Agile Testing Quadrants', originally defined by Brian Marick.

Figure 7.5 proposes a simple-to-understand model of what is included in Agile testing. It gives guidance on the types of testing that may be used in an Agile delivery, as well as what the testing should focus on and how it should be delivered.

Figure 7.5 Agile testing quadrants

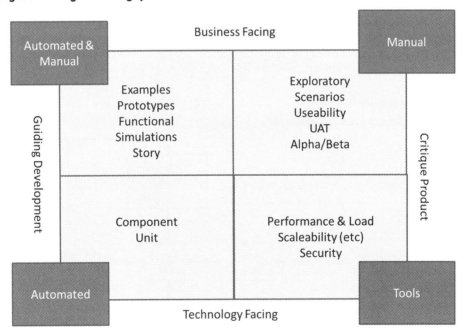

There are a number of testing-based development practices that are typically used in Agile deliveries. These are described in the following sections.

7.4.1 Agile testing practices

7.4.1.1 TFD (Test First Development)

As the name suggests this practice means that tests are written before any development or coding to meet story acceptance criteria happens. When a story is to be developed, team members with analysis and design, build and test skills (an approach sometimes called 'The Three Amigos' (Hewitt, 2013)) get together and develop the tests, edge cases and so on just prior to delivery.

Where it is practical the customer will also be involved in creating tests so that they have confidence that the tests will prove that the acceptance criteria are met.

Once the tests have been written, a test–build cycle (test, then build, then test, then build etc., up to the point all tests are passed) is implemented until any and all bugs associated with the build have been fixed and the customer is happy to sign the story off as 'done'.

TFD validates that what has been built meets the story acceptance criteria (via the tests) agreed by the customer.

7.4.1.2 TDD (Test Driven Development)

Test Driven Development (Beck, 2002) is normally implemented at the unit or component testing level. In essence it is a style of TFD; the main difference is that TDD normally includes the Agile practice of 'refactoring' (see Section 8.10).

TDD validates that what has been built passes the tests and therefore meets the acceptance criteria upon which the tests are based, and that the design is appropriate with minimal technical debt. The TDD development cycle (sometimes known as 'red-green-refactor') is shown in Figure 7.6:

Figure 7.6 Test Driven Development

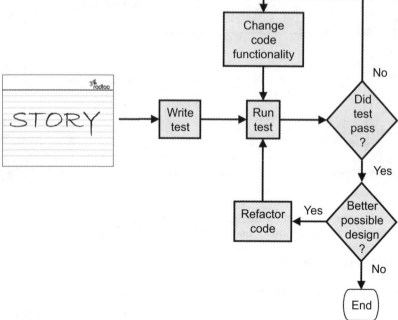

The benefits of TDD are numerous:

- Good design principles need to be followed to test code in isolation.
- The speed of the test–code cycle (enabled by automated testing tools) enables fast refactoring and therefore is a big enabler of emergent design (see Section 9.2).
- The focus is on the interface of the code.
- The unit test documents the expected behaviour of the code.
- The unit test is repeatable and can be automated.

In TDD, the team focuses on conditions in the test that could cause the code to fail. Once there are no more failure conditions, the development is said to be complete. Automated tests (see Section 8.10) give the team the confidence that the system operates as expected. As new stories are added, existing tests will quickly identify any unexpected issues. The focus in TDD is on design and ensuring that products are designed in a fit-for-purpose way.

7.4.1.3 ATDD (Acceptance Test Driven Development)

Acceptance Test Driven Development (Pugh, 2011) is very similar to TDD, although it is closer to user acceptance testing (UAT). While it is an effective approach to testing, many organisations prefer to use behaviour-driven development (see section 7.4.1.4); therefore this book does not expand upon ATDD any further.

7.4.1.4 BDD (Behaviour Driven Development)

Behaviour Driven Development (North, 2006) focuses on scenario testing to make sure that the system behaves in the way the user expects it to behave. In this, BDD goes beyond simply delivering software that works and is designed well; it provides a very effective bridge between people with analytical, design, coding and testing skills because it encourages them to work together as a team rather than just passing documents to each other.

A detailed description of how to write story acceptance criteria related to BDD may be found in Section 7.1.2.

All of the practices described above rely on automated testing and effective continuous integration (see Section 8.10.2).

7.4.1.5 Specification by example

Specification by example (Adzic, 2010) and (Fowler, 2011) ensures that what is being created matches the customer's requirements and that testing is focused on the parts of the system that create the greatest business value. Gojko Adzic defines specification by example as

> ... a set of process patterns that facilitate change in software products to ensure that the right product is delivered efficiently. When I say the right product, I mean software that delivers the required business effect or fulfills a business goal set by

the customers or business users and it is flexible enough to be able to receive future improvements with a relatively flat cost of change.

(Adzic, 2010)

There are a number of key elements to specification by example:

- deriving system scope from business goals that are clearly expressed and understood by the customer and stakeholders;
- specifying acceptance criteria for stories collaboratively between team, customer and stakeholder, as well as agreeing appropriate levels of testing detail;
- illustrating and agreeing requirements using examples (the team may add more detail in relation to edge cases where required);
- refining specifications throughout the lifetime of the product;
- automating validation without changing specifications;
- validating frequently that the product being built meets the specifications;
- evolving a documentation system that consists of simple-to-understand requirements and tests that prove them.

8 COMMON AGILE PRACTICES

In this Chapter we detail the main Agile practices that are generic across most or all frameworks.

8.1 SHORT FEEDBACK LOOPS

Feedback loops are critical to the success of an Agile delivery. An empirical process is one where a team inspect how and what they have done, and use this feedback to improve their process and products – this is called a feedback loop (see Figure 8.1).

Figure 8.1 Feedback loops

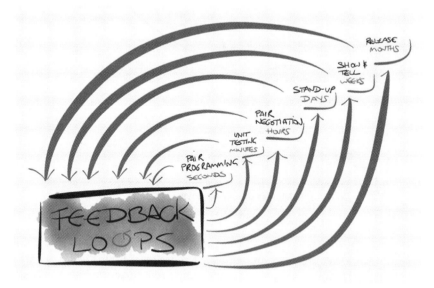

The following are some examples of feedback loops:

- Face-to-face conversations (see Section 8.2).
- Daily stand-ups (see Section 8.3).
- Show and tells (see Section 8.4).

Other forms of feedback loops, such as pair programming (Section 14.1), unit testing and continuous integration (Section 8.10) and regular releases (Section 10.2) are covered later in the book.

8.2 FACE-TO-FACE COMMUNICATION

Face-to-face communication enables fast feedback loops and adds rich non-verbal communication to any interaction. It also solidifies relationships, creates mutual trust and defines centres of influence within an organisation.

Figure 8.2 shows the relationship between the communication channel being used and the effectiveness and richness of communication (Ambler, 2001–14)

Figure 8.2 Richness of communication channels

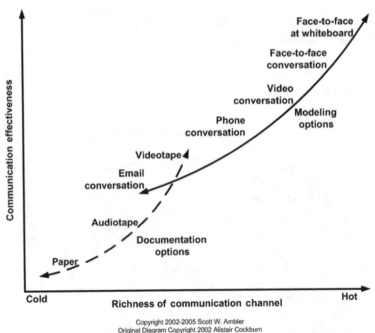

Copyright 2002-2005 Scott W. Ambler
Original Diagram Copyright 2002 Alistair Cockburn

In collaborative work, face-to-face interaction is a more favourable choice, in particular if a relatively more difficult and significant task is involved – discovery sessions, kick-off meetings and contract negotiations rarely take place via mediated communication such as audio, video, email and so on.

In Agile deliveries, it is recommended that teams are physically co-located to enable face-to-face communications and the benefits it brings. In the next sections we will discuss why face-to-face communications are key to enable Agile delivery and how to facilitate it for distributed teams.

Number of communication channels

The more people are involved in a communication, the more difficult it becomes to communicate effectively. To highlight this communication challenge, Kerzner (2013) looks at how the number of communication lines (channels) within a defined group of people affects communication. As shown in the table below, the number of communication channels increases disproportionally to the number of people in a group.

People	2	3	4	5	6	7	8	9	10
Channels	1	3	6	10	15	21	28	36	45

This is why Agile teams tend to consist of between 3 (to enable team dynamics) and 11 members (to restrict communication channels to a manageable size face-to-face).

Team proximity

In spite of promising technology achievements, such as high-resolution video conferencing at affordable cost, project management platforms and mobile phone applications, proximity still tends to be the preferred viable option for effective collaboration.

Figure 8.3 shows the impact of proximity on effective communication (Ambler, 2001–14). Proximity generates spontaneous, memorable and sustainable interactions, as it provides numerous unscheduled opportunities that can lead to conversation: in designated recreation areas, in the office kitchen or in lifts. Such interactions, known as 'water cooler conversations', have powerful effects on decision making, conformity, social pressure and familiarity. The 'mere exposure effect' (Zajonc, 1968) can facilitate problem solving, product development and task coordination.

Figure 8.3 Effects of proximity

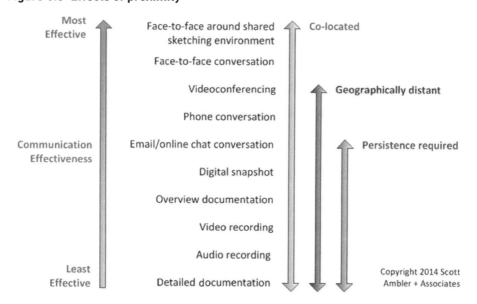

Copyright 2014 Scott Ambler + Associates

The frequency of spontaneous communication is predominantly correlated with office distance, with frequency dropping exponentially as the distance between the two collaborators increases.

In early collaborative studies of competitive games (Deutsch, 1958), participants were strongly advised to 'win as much as they could for themselves' when competing against their opponent. Observations showed that 71 per cent of participating 'couples' made cooperative choices for a common cause in cases where communication was allowed. In trials during which communication was strictly prohibited, only 36 per cent of participants fought for a common goal. Evidently, such behaviour derives from the silent commitment imposed by face-to-face social contracts, in addition to the group identity that is formed through face-to-face interactions.

Osmotic communication

This term was introduced by Alistair Cockburn (Cockburn, 2004) and refers to the boundaryless information flows amongst co-located team members as part of their daily conversations and interactions. For instance, two colleagues engage in conversation about exploring a solution to a complex problem. Another team member overhears the discussion and, in order to provide her colleagues with an alternative solution – which could potentially be the solution that they are looking for – she decides to join in the conversation. Such interaction would not be possible in distant collaboration.

Tacit knowledge

Tacit knowledge is knowledge that cannot be codified, is difficult to communicate in written form and is normally communicated face-to-face. Tacit knowledge can be individual tacit knowledge or group tacit knowledge.

At the individual level, tacit knowledge is closely related to the concept of accumulative knowledge, based on a plethora of real-life events. It is knowledge that is derived from the stock of learning activities and is expressed in public through skills. At the group level, team knowledge is based on common experiences.

8.2.1 Distributed team communication challenges

There are two main types of non-physically located teams:

- **Multisite team** This refers to one product group that is split up across various locations into smaller teams.
- **Distributed team** This means that individual team members are located at different sites.

It is worth noting that geographic dispersion is not limited to different offices, countries or continents – it can happen in the same office, within rooms (with space dividers), between different rooms (with physical walls) or between floors.

The primary economic driver to embrace distributed or multisite teams, in particular in the context of offshoring, is to minimise operational cost. Beyond apparent financial gains, organisations benefit from offshoring due to new innovation, speed, agility and new revenue opportunities (Carmel and Tija, 2005). However, this geographic dispersion brings with it the communication challenges of distance and time, which cannot be completely eliminated.

8.2.1.1 Five centrifugal forces of distributed teams

The virtual distance amongst knowledge workers can be further analysed by looking at the following five centrifugal forces of distributed teams (Carmel and Tija, 2005).

Force 1: Communication breakdown In any face-to-face communication, humans interpret body language (kinesics), voice (paralanguage), touch (haptics), distance (proxemics) and environmental characteristics. It is believed that 80 per cent of exchanged messages are non-verbal, including voice quality, rate, pitch, volume, accent, blink rate, hand gestures, eye contact, mouth gestures and so on. It is more difficult to enable effective communication with geographically dispersed teams because none of these elements are easily put in place.

Force 2: Coordination breakdown Agile development relies on frequent inspection and adaptation. Through face-to-face interactions, teams make decisions on adjustments to realign the product increment with the overall objective in the following iteration/sprint. These decisions are often based on numerous ad-hoc conversations around small adjustments: brief discussions about design and architecture, requests for clarification on user experience, questions about the product vision and so forth. If team members are located in close proximity, such conversations can occur spontaneously; if this proximity is missing then there is a significant risk of coordination breakdown.

Force 3: Loss of communication richness Distributed environments tend to lack communication richness. This introduces various challenges and negatively influences the success of interactions: messages might only be partially transmitted, acknowledged (in absence of non-verbal cues) and partially understood (for example, due to being unable to immediately interact with the transmitter and ask for clarification). Messages with missing information often lead to actions that are misaligned with the goal, delays (for example, due to asynchronous receipt of messages; time zone differences; need for clarifications), rework (for example, due to lack of deep understanding) and conflict (because of the emotional involvement of the team members).

Force 4: Loss of team bonding Face-to-face communication is a vital element in team bonding and establishing trust among team members. Trust, in turn, is a significant contributor to team productivity and job satisfaction. In distributed environments, it is often challenging to establish trust amongst the team unless some prior working relationships exist. This leads to distributed teams lacking cohesion and, in the worst case, to mistrust, which will have a disastrous effect on teams.

Force 5: Cultural differences In particular when offshoring it is likely that teams will be made up of people from different cultures and backgrounds. Lack of cultural understanding is often a factor that introduces conflict and mistrust, which will lead to project failure.

According to Hofstede (1994), cross-cultural communication is prone to misinterpretation, as transmitter and receiver comprehend the same verbal and non-verbal message differently. Face-to-face communication builds an environment of trust, and is therefore less likely to be misinterpreted and more likely to foster cultural understanding.

The challenges listed above can be further exacerbated if utilising more traditional delivery approaches that rely on documentation for communication. When communication is already a significant issue, then just passing very detailed documents between team members runs the risk of making communication issues significantly worse, mainly because of the risk of misinterpretation.

8.2.2 Distributed team communication risk mitigation

Due to the issues discussed above, replicating the benefits of face-to-face communication in distributed teams presents numerous challenges. The following virtual co-location tools can help to mitigate the impact:

- **Video conferencing** Building rapport and eliminating barriers between teams, such as the subtle us–them attitude, is achievable through video communications as it allows members to pick up on non-verbal cues. Video conferencing is ideal for daily stand-up meetings, sprint reviews and retrospectives. For distributed teams it is recommended to engage in video sessions as frequently as possible.

- **Knowledge management systems** Creating a knowledge cube (see Chapter 5) of organisational knowledge that contains data from the broader spectrum of the business, be it finance, marketing, product, software engineering and so on, can be particularly beneficial for productivity and boundaryless information flow. It provides a go-to place for continuous reference to explicit knowledge.

- **Collaboration platforms** Distributed development and everyday collaboration is frequently reliant on the extensive use of collaboration platforms. A unified communication approach involves task-oriented communication, with comments, discussion boards and file transfer capabilities related to specific work items. It also gives Agile leads, customers, the team and other stakeholders better visibility of the status of work, with transparency of all communications.

- **Instant messaging (IM)** This tool can help to replicate spontaneous communication up to a certain extent. It is particularly useful for short questions and requests for brief clarifications. Instant messaging virtually brings co-workers closer, though it cannot fully replace the benefits of face-to-face communication.

- **Interactive whiteboards** Interactive whiteboards can prove useful especially in design and architecture sessions that have to take place remotely. Whiteboard content can be shared in real-time across multiple locations, allowing distributed participants to collaborate using inclusive techniques, such as drawings, diagrams, low-fidelity user interface wireframes, and other forms of Agile modelling.

8.2.2.1 Cross-pollination

Cross-pollination is based on mobilising resources from one development site to the other. Especially during project kick-off activities, it is important to create a platform for face-to-face group workshops, pair programming sessions and so on. Resources should not be limited to the management level because communication needs to happen across the whole team. All team members should be an essential part of cross-pollination, allowing them to interact with business and decision-making stakeholders.

8.3 DAILY STAND-UPS

Daily stand-ups (or daily synchronisation meetings) are, as the name suggests, daily meetings that allow a team to inspect the progress that has been achieved, and then plan out the day's work, including any corrective actions needed to ensure that the best results obtainable during the iteration are delivered.

The meetings should be limited to a maximum of 15 minutes. One way to achieve this is for the attendees to remain standing (which is why it is called the 'daily stand-up'). If an issue arises that requires more discussion, then it should be discussed by the affected team members in a separate meeting, which should be held immediately afterwards.

Daily stand-ups are not a project management or progress update meeting; instead the focus is on synchronisation within the team. Usually these meetings follow a very simple format, with each team member answering each one of the following three questions:

- What did I do yesterday that helped the team meet the sprint/iteration goal?
- What will I do today to help the team meet the sprint/iteration goal?
- Do I see any impediment that prevents me or the team from meeting the sprint/iteration goal?

An alternative to this approach, which works well for teams who are focused on keeping a continuous flow of work that is balanced across everyone in the team, is to 'walk the board' – a reference to the visual board around which these meetings are normally centred (see Section 8.7).

In this approach (assuming tasks flow from left to right on the visual board), a team would start from the rightmost point on the board and talk about the tasks (and/or stories) that are nearest completion. Then they work their way back across the board. This method is based on the assumption that it is most important to complete the tasks that are nearest to completion as they would be the highest value ones.

The best time of day to hold a daily stand-up is about 30 minutes into the working day. This allows team members to arrive at their desks and refresh their memory of the previous day before attending the meeting. The daily stand-up will then give them their priority work for the day.

Of course, this is an ideal that won't suit every team – for example, if some team members work in different locations or even different countries, then the timing of the meeting should be set so everyone can attend. Including remote teams or workers in a stand-up meeting can prove problematic as not everyone might be able to see or have access to the visual board, which provides a common reference point. Fortunately software tools can help manage the board so all team members can see it and video streaming technology can allow all team members to see each other and a physical board at the meeting.

8.4 SHOW AND TELLS

'Show and tells' are meetings that are typically held at the end of a sprint/iteration and / or release (see Section 5.1). They are an essential part of the Agile inspect-and-adapt cycle.

The purpose of these meetings is for the team to demonstrate to the stakeholders all stories completed during an iteration/sprint, to seek immediate feedback from the stakeholders, as well as get recognition for their work. This means that all available stakeholders and all team members should attend show and tells.

Show and tells should be live demonstrations of a new working product or feature as it is essential that stakeholders get to see, touch and feel the real product. A show and tell that uses screenshots, simulations or models of the product will not add as much value as a demonstration of real working software; only by seeing the real working product can the stakeholders be able to provide useful and accurate feedback.

The person who demonstrates a product depends on each team's circumstances. For example, more experienced team members or those people who are comfortable speaking in front of an audience may present. Some teams may pick the same person to run the demonstration every iteration/sprint for a consistent approach. Other teams may rotate the job to ensure everyone has an opportunity to run the demonstration should they so wish.

Alternatively, if a team has a very engaged customer, having the customer do the demonstration adds a lot of gravitas as it is essentially a presentation 'from business person to business person'. In all circumstances it is bad practice to only show completed stories to the customer at a show and tell, because if the customer starts highlighting that the stories are incorrect at this late point it sends a very negative message to other stakeholders who are in attendance.

Show and tell meetings should also provide the opportunity to identify stories that were planned but not completed within the iteration/sprint, and to agree a date when they will be achieved. They can also be a good time to highlight risks, issues, blockers and assumptions the team are working with as stakeholders may offer good insight and information that may assist with the resolution of these. Any defects of the product that have been identified should also be shared.

Teams should avoid presenting stories that are only nearly complete at 'show and tell' meetings as this can give stakeholders the false impression that stories are more advanced in their development than they truly are.

Some up-front preparation is needed for show and tell meetings. For example the product needs to be doubled-checked to ensure all its new stories are working in the environment where the demonstration will take place. The team also need to prepare the location for the show and tell and check the facilities such as network communications. It can also be useful to rehearse the demonstration in the place where it will happen. After the meeting any output should be fed into the backlog and prioritised potentially for development during the next time-box.

8.5 RETROSPECTIVES

Traditionally, project management has embraced the concept of lessons learnt and post-mortem meetings, which capture the learning outcomes of a project, post completion or termination. Such lessons would be shared with the rest of the organisation to consider in future projects that exhibit common characteristics, for example, similar business requirements, technical domain, team structures, collaboration dynamics.

Retrospectives provide opportunities for the team and others to specifically focus on inspecting and adapting what they do and how they do it. The purpose of retrospectives is to continually improve the product as it is being delivered and to continuously improve how the products are delivered. Teams should analyse how well they performed by identifying things that have worked well and those that could be improved. Retrospectives are a key element to fulfil the continuous improvement mentality.

Retrospectives are most commonly scheduled at the end of each sprint/iteration, although they should not be limited to this – they should also be held at any other appropriate point if required, for example, after a release has been completed or following issues that may have occurred.

There are many different types of retrospectives, depending on what the team are reflecting upon and adjusting, and there are many different techniques that can be used. For example, at the end of the sprint/iteration time-box the team will typically spend a few hours considering:

- What went well?
- What didn't go well?
- What are we going to do differently next time?

Figure 8.4 shows a typical retrospective cycle, from the delivery of an iteration/sprint through to the retrospective.

Figure 8.4 Agile retrospective process

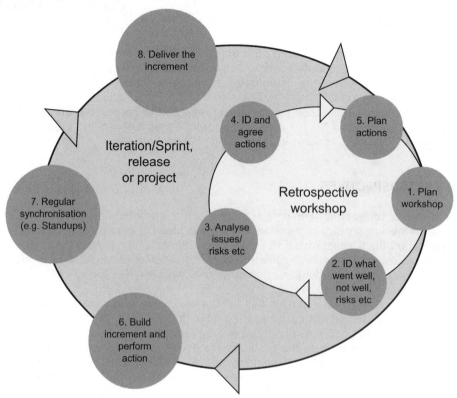

- **Plan workshop** Give some background about why the retrospective is being performed, how the workshop objectives are going to be met and what it is the team are going to do. This may be described in a workshop agenda that is sent out prior to the retrospective workshop.

- **Identify what went well, what didn't go well, risks and so on** There are numerous ways to do this, and usually using some type of 'brainstorming' technique works well. The focus here is on understanding what will be discussed in this retrospective workshop. It is important to keep in mind that it is as important to celebrate success (what went well) as it is to understand what didn't go well.

- **Analyse issues** There are numerous ways to generate insights depending on what the retrospective is focused on. A few retrospective activities will be discussed in Section 8.5.1. Also review issues and actions that have been raised in previous retrospectives.

- **Identify and agree actions** Identify actions as required and agree within the team that the focus within the next iteration/sprint, release or project will be on these actions.

- **Build increment and perform actions** Build the next increment of the product and deliver the actions that were agreed upon in the last retrospective.

- **Regular synchronisation** Synchronise regularly to ensure that the actions are on track.
- **Deliver the increment** Deliver the product increment from the iteration, including any actions agreed from the last retrospective.
- **Deliver the cycle again** Kaizen or continuous improvement.

The insights gathered in a retrospective can be of use to the existing project, business domain, technical domain and team, and the added-value knowledge can be applied in subsequent iterations/sprints.

Retrospectives generate a number of action points, which should contribute to and improve the following aspects:

- collaboration;
- productivity;
- quality;
- capability;
- capacity;
- team dynamics.

The team should also reflect on how they work together and how they interact with the rest of the business as a team. Regarding their productivity, the team should identify opportunities to reduce rework to allow for more productive work to be done.

Quality should be a constant focus throughout an Agile delivery. Therefore, the team should assess their approach to delivering better code with fewer defects. Also, the team should focus on improving their capacity by identifying efficiency improvements. Finally, close collaboration may introduce friction and conflict, and retrospectives are an appropriate time to express concerns and emotions and discuss possible resolutions.

Facilitating retrospectives

It is usually the Agile lead (see Section 6.3) who acts as a facilitator in a retrospective and encourages team members to commit to a list of action points. During retrospectives, it is important to make sure that the team identify things that are within their sphere of influence, rather than concentrating on the ones that will change the world or reinvent the wheel.

There is also the danger that team members may air all of their more petty grumbles (like 'the coffee isn't nice enough'). These grumbles might be acceptable the first time they are raised and can be passed onto the person responsible; however, it is important to move on from this and help the team to identify things that improve their process, tools, culture, ways of working and so on.

If retrospectives are run in the same format all the time every time, teams might become bored, which in turn will make the meeting ineffective. Some measures to counteract this are to change location or to vary the formality of the meetings.

8.5.1 Examples of retrospective activities

8.5.1.1 Explorers/Shoppers/Vacationers/Prisoners

Over time, team engagement towards the retrospectives may diminish for a variety of reasons. To discuss the underlying reasons behind low engagement, a facilitator asks the team members to associate themselves with one of the following behaviours:

- **Explorers:** eager to discover new ideas and insights, with desire to gather all available information about the iteration/release/project;
- **Shoppers:** willing to expose themselves to available information and select one useful new idea;
- **Vacationers:** no interest in the works of the retrospective, but happy to be away from their desk;
- **Prisoners:** feel forced to attend and would prefer to be elsewhere.

The facilitator can then assess if the style or focus of the retrospective needs to change.

8.5.1.2 Timeline

At times, teams can be called to identify the root cause of an issue and its progression before taking any action. In the timeline technique, a facilitator draws a timeline on a whiteboard, which represents the period under review. The participants are asked to write events on coloured sticky notes, in the form of good, problematic, and significant. Following that, they are called to mount them on the whiteboard in relation to the timeline. The exercise provides the team with better insights into the root cause of problems, allowing them to reflect and understand how to avoid similar situations in a future iteration.

8.5.1.3 Five whys

The five whys exercise deals with causation, i.e., the relationship between an event (cause) and another event (effect). It helps identify the true root cause of a problem by asking why repetitively and bypassing evident answers that do not shed light on the investigation. Here is an example:

> Event: The team can never focus on delivery and is therefore failing to deliver iteration/sprint goals.
>
> Why: Management keep interrupting the team.
>
> Why: Management keep asking for progress updates.
>
> Why: They can't see the daily status of the iteration/sprint and don't know if the team are on track.
>
> Why: The burn-down chart is always out of date and doesn't show the accurate delivery status.
>
> Why: The burn-down chart isn't being updated daily by the team.

8.5.1.4 Fishbone diagram

A fishbone diagram provides a visual approach to help with root cause analysis of problems, showing them alongside their contributing factors. A facilitator draws a simplified fishbone diagram on a whiteboard, placing the problem at the head. In a collaborative manner, the participants identify the contributing factors, for which the five whys exercise can be used. Alternatively, the factors can be related to common cause areas, such as people, procedure, policies, place, systems, suppliers, skills and surroundings. As the categories are written on the diagram, the team needs to assign and write the causes of the effect under the appropriate category; they then define actions to treat, terminate, tolerate or transfer the cause.

8.5.1.5 Plus/delta

This feedback technique, which identifies positives as well as the negatives of an event, gives team members the opportunity to discuss the practices, ideas and patterns that have a positive effect on their collaboration and delivery, as well as reflect on those elements that require improvement or adjustment.

8.6 EMERGENT DOCUMENTATION

In an Agile delivery the focus is on producing only the relevant documentation in line with the emergence of the system. Documentation should only be produced if and when it adds value, and should always be fit for purpose, i.e. suitable for the audience.

It can be tempting to miss out documentation tasks as it is often not the most exciting part of the job, so teams need to find a way to make sure documentation is kept up to date. The easiest way to do this is to specifically make documentation production a standard part of the definition of 'done' (see Section 10.2.1) or have specific stories in place to create appropriate documents, or add documents as acceptance criteria on some stories. This means that before any piece of work can be signed off as complete, the necessary documentation has to be completed as well.

Typical types of IT systems documentation include:

- design documentation;
- code documentation;
- test documentation;
- business user documentation;
- operational documentation.

There are some occasions when it is necessary to produce documentation in advance of product development. For example, sometimes there may be a regulatory or commercial reason to produce a document or a specification for an interface that will enable an external team to develop something that will interact with the product that is being developed.

Design documentation

In Agile there is generally no specific guidance on what design documentation should be produced. Generally the team will inspect and adapt to produce whatever design documentation adds value. However, in the majority of cases there will need to be some design documentation to ensure that the product can be effectively supported and maintained throughout its lifetime.

A key concept in Agile is emergent or opportunistic design, meaning that the design evolves as the team learn via the inspect and adapt cycles. The implication for design documentation therefore is to not try to define everything up front as this will restrict the ability to implement design in an emergent way.

This is easy when there are only one or two teams working on a product. However, once a product has multiple teams working on it there is typically a need to ensure that all teams are working towards the same design pattern. In this case high-level foundation design principles may need to be documented. The principles should not be a complete product design document; rather they should contain enough detail for the teams to work on for the next couple of iterations/sprints (or whatever time period is appropriate). This is called EDUF (enough design up front – (DSDM Consortium, 2014b)). It focuses the teams to work towards an intentional design, yet avoids wasting effort creating a fully completed design document up front.

Code as documentation

Code written by a team should be self-documenting, meaning it should be written in a way that is easy to understand by anyone, making extra documentation unnecessary. This can be achieved either by adding clear comments within the code or by ensuring the code is so simple and clear that its intent is obvious.

Focusing on simplicity of code aligns to the software craftsmanship movement (Software Craftsmanship, 2009), which states that a software craftsman will create self-documenting, simple-to-understand code that is easy to maintain in the future. If code does need explaining then this is a 'code smell' (Fowler et al., 1999) and requires refactoring (see Section 8.10.1).

Test documentation

Test documentation (e.g., test strategy, test scripts and so on) should be produced to support whatever testing is being implemented, (see Section 7.4).

Test documentation can also be used to provide a specification of the system (for examples see 'specification by example' and 'Behaviour Driven Development' (Section 7.4.1).

Business user documentation

Business user documentation is there to aid users of a system to use the system effectively. It may be online help, supporting documentation or whatever is fit for purpose. Some IT products do not require business user documentation, as the interface is specifically designed to be very easy to use. Other technology products do require business user documentation and where this is the case the documentation is core to the delivery. There is no specific guidance about what business documentation should be produced in an Agile delivery; instead, the focus is on developing fit-for-purpose business documentation as the product emerges.

Operational documentation

If a system is put into an environment that is controlled by a separate operational team, it is highly likely that documentation to describe the system to a level that the support team can support it will be required. Appropriate documentation needs to be inspected and adapted based on the operational team's requirements. Therefore it is essential that the operational team is considered a key stakeholder and that stories are created that represent their requirements.

8.7 VISUAL BOARDS

8.7.1 Information radiator

An 'information radiator', as shown in Figure 8.5, is intended to be openly visible and available, 'radiating' information to everyone who sees it. The use of information radiators is a great way of conveying information about the current state of a delivery.

Figure 8.5 Information radiator

Information radiators can be either physical, for example on a wall, whiteboard or similar, or virtual, for example, as part of an Agile software planning tool. Many people still prefer to use physical boards as it allows direct interaction; for example, a team member can pick up a story or task card that represents what they are working on and physically move/progress it once the work is complete. This generally offers much more satisfaction than just changing a virtual ticket status. It is also immediately visible to everyone that progress has been made, without the need to access a piece of software.

However, there are limitations to the use of a physical board. For example, if a team is distributed across different countries, offices or even different rooms, team members may not be able to see and interact with a physical board in a single location. In such cases, visual boards held in the virtual world can be extremely useful; however, Agile teams sometimes refer to these as 'information refrigerators' as there's the risk that no one ever keeps them up to date.

Information radiators are a key source of information for daily stand-up meetings, show and tells and retrospectives. For example, at a daily stand-up team members can talk about the progress made on stories and tasks represented on the board. For a show and tell, visual boards provide information on completed stories and tasks. For a retrospective, boards can show information that might need attention, for example tasks that have been blocked, or tasks that have been on the board for a long time.

As a minimum any information radiator should show the current state of tasks/stories a team are working on and how far they have to go to get to 'done' status. However, it can also include other information, for example, who is currently working on what task(s).

It can also show a burn-down chart, a burn-up diagram, blockers list or project information such as the key items from the risks assumptions issues and dependencies (RAID) log.

> The only person who can move a story to complete status (meaning the acceptance criteria are now at 'done' status) on a visual board is the customer.

8.7.2 Burn-down chart

A burn-down chart normally compares planned effort left to complete a task against the actual effort left. It works well for a team who have estimated the effort required to complete tasks within an iteration/sprint in hours. Initially the chart would show the predicted rate at which a delivery will occur by forecasting how much effort (in hours) should be left on a particular day within the sprint/iteration. This is plotted as a line on the chart. On a daily basis each team member then updates how much effort they actually have left against the tasks they are delivering, and the total of the latest estimated hours left is then plotted onto the chart each day. The two lines should be broadly following each other through the iteration/sprint.

The following example relates to a single iteration/sprint where it would be usual to use hours as a measure of effort.

A burn-down chart (Figure 8.6) can be used to predict whether a team will succeed in delivering everything within the iteration/sprint by extrapolating the 'actual effort left' line based on latest forecasts. When properly planned, the chart should show that all the work will be done just before the end of the sprint/iteration.

Figure 8.6 Burn-down chart - example 1

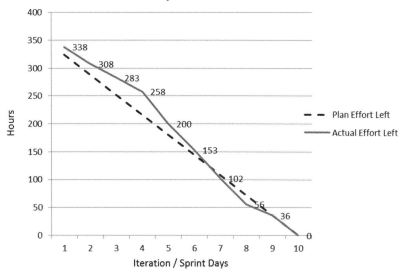

Story completion (measured in story points) can also be used for iteration/sprint burn-down; however, this is likely to create a chart that is not granular enough for effective measurement of progress. Release or project burn-down charts are also typically created and in those cases forecast and actual story point burn-downs would be used.

8.7.3 Burn-up Chart

A burn-up chart (Figure 8.7) monitors the total work required, normally in hours or story points, and then displays the actual work completed; where the two lines intersect the iteration/sprint is 'done'.

Figure 8.7 Burn-up chart - example 2

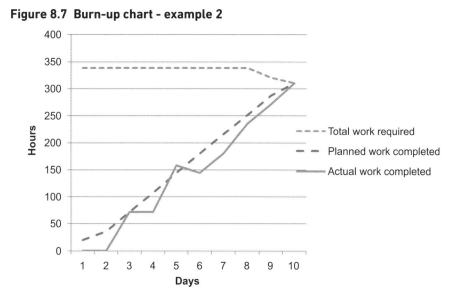

Typically a 'planned work completed' line is also added to the burn-up chart.

8.7.4 RAID log

A RAID log is a single repository of all key information about a delivery that is not expressed on the backlog or in other documentation. 'RAID' stands for:

- Risks.
- Assumptions.
- Issues/actions.
- Decisions (or dependencies).

Displaying the major RAID log items on the visual board can be very useful to provide a quick, visual overview of risks and so on, though it is important not to 'overload' the board with information. The best approach is to only flag RAID items that are, or could be, impacting on what the team is doing within the current sprint/iteration or release.

8.8 SUSTAINABLE PACE

Sustainable pace is one of the practices that was introduced into Agile by eXtreme Programming (XP) (see Section 14.1). eXtreme Programming advocates frequent 'releases' in short development cycles. This is intended to improve productivity and introduce checkpoints at which new customer requirements can be adopted.

In the early 1900s, Ford Motor Company ran dozens of tests to discover the optimum work hours for worker productivity. They discovered that the 'sweet spot' is 40 hours a week and that, while adding another 20 hours provides a minor increase in productivity, this increase only lasts for 3 to 4 weeks, and then turns negative (James, 2012).

Research by the Roundtable (Holloway Consulting, 2014) in the 1980s found that you could get short-term gains by going to 60- or 70-hour weeks very briefly – for example, pushing extra hard for a few weeks to meet a critical production deadline. However, increasing a team's hours in the office by 50 per cent (from 40 to 60 hours) does not result in 50 per cent more output. In fact, the numbers may typically be something closer to 25–30 per cent more work in 50 per cent more time.

This is because by the eighth hour of the day, people's best work is usually already behind them (typically turned in between hours two and six). In hour nine, as fatigue sets in, they're only going to deliver a fraction of their usual capacity. And with every extra hour beyond that, the workers' productivity levels continue to drop, until at around 10 or 12 hours they hit full exhaustion.

Overtime is only effective over very short periods of time. This is because daily productivity starts falling off in the second week, and declines rapidly with every successive week as burnout sets in (Chapman, 1909).

> **Burnout** is a psychological term that refers to long-term exhaustion and diminished interest in work. Tired teams will make more mistakes, produce more defects, deliver less and with a reduced quality level. Indeed, burnout could ultimately lead to a team member deciding to leave the organisation.

Additionally working a lot of overtime creates a level of burnout that sets in far sooner, is far more acute, and requires much more to fix than most managers or workers think it does.

> Working overtime sucks the spirit and motivation out of your team. When your team becomes tired and demoralized they will get less work done, not more, no matter how many hours are worked. Becoming over-worked today steals development progress from the future.

(Wells, 2009)

8.9 FOCUS ON QUALITY

This section looks at the concept of quality in an Agile context and gives an overview of the main quality focus practices.

8.9.1 Functional quality

Ensuring functional quality is about delivering the features and functionality the customer wants. Lack of functional quality, in other words not delivering the system the customer wants, is a common criticism levelled at IT deliveries.

Customer collaboration, one of the four Agile Manifesto statements is a key focus of ensuring functional quality. It feeds into defining acceptance criteria for each feature, the review of stories throughout development and at the end of development, as well as into the definition of 'done' (see Section 10.2).

8.9.2 Technical quality

There are some practices used specifically in software development that are aimed at ensuring that software is of an appropriate level of technical quality. The ones listed below are the foundation technical quality practices that are expected to be in place in any Agile team, and will be covered in more detail in Section 8.10. For a description of other more technically biased practices that may be implemented see eXtreme Programming (Section 14.1).

- **Refactoring** – this is changing the design of a system without changing its behaviour.
- **Continuous integration** – this is about continuously ensuring that everything works together in an integrated way.

- **Test Driven Development** – Test Driven Development (TDD) is a practice where test cases are written before the actual functionality is developed. Tests are written for each unit/component of code.

8.10 MAJOR AGILE TECHNICAL PRACTICES

This section provides a foundation-level understanding of some of the major Agile technical practices. A more exhaustive list of technical practices may be found in the description of eXtreme Programming in Section 14.1.

8.10.1 Refactoring

Refactoring (Fowler et al., 1999) is changing the design of a system without changing its behaviour. It is used to create a design and architecture for a product that is fit for purpose and doesn't contain technical debt (see Section 10.4.1).

Teams need to have confidence that, as they develop the system design (see Section 9.2), they can revisit the design and architecture and make changes based on learning. Refactoring is specifically focused on improving and ensuring continual quality of the design of the system (including the database), and should be done as a matter of normal development practice to prevent the software becoming laden with technical debt. Continual attention to refactoring ensures that the code is of good design and easily maintainable. Code that is easy to maintain will produce fewer defects and ensure that systems are easy to support and maintain.

One way to implement refactoring is Test Driven Development (TDD – see Section 7.4.1.2).

An analogy to explain refactoring is that, when camping, it is good etiquette to leave the campsite in as good or better condition than when you arrived. The same applies to software development: when a developer designs and implements a new feature, it is good practice to make sure the surrounding code, tables, documentation and so on are still in good shape.

When refactoring, it is important to have a suite of tests which should be executed before anything is refactored to ensure they are running correctly. After refactoring has been completed the tests should be run again to ensure there has been no adverse effect. This ability is closely aligned with the concept of continuous integration.

8.10.2 Continuous integration and automated testing

Not integrating testing throughout the software development lifecycle poses a very significant risk as it unnecessarily extends feedback loops (see Section 8.1). A nightmare scenario is that important testing is only performed at the end of a release or project, and if at that point a significant problem is found nothing can be done about it without extending timescale and costs.

Therefore Agile deliveries implement continuous integration (Fowler, n.d.), which means that any change to a product will initiate full regression tests of the whole product (i.e. tests to ensure that adding something has not caused the overall software environment to break).

Continuous integration enables team members to frequently and independently integrate their work with the core product and therefore ensure that the overall product continues to work in an integrated manner. Typically team members will integrate their work multiple times a day, and at the very least on a daily basis. The integrated work is continually verified by build and test software tools. This gives the team confidence that the system works in an integrated way in any environment (e.g. an integration test environment), and that they will not hit a significant blocker late in the development cycle by discovering an integration problem.

There are a number of principles associated with continuous integration:

- Maintain a central source control system.
- Automate the build (see Section 8.10.3).
- Make the build self-testing – automated regression tests.
- Everyone commits to the code baseline every day.
- The code baseline is rebuilt every day (at least).
- Builds must be fast – especially if building multiple times a day.
- Test in environments that mirror the live environments wherever possible.
- Everyone can easily see the latest product (build).
- Everyone can easily see the results of builds – the focus of the team is to fix broken builds as soon as possible.
- Automate deployment where possible.

Teams should always be working on the latest version of a product. They should regularly pull the latest changes from the central source control system and then check-in their updated code. New code check-ins are detected by the continuous integration system. The system will then run a process to rebuild the changed software environment, and run unit and integration tests to see if anything has regressed. If there are any tests that fail, then the build fails and the developer who checked-in the code will be notified by the system. It is then the responsibility of the developer who changed the code to resolve the problem on behalf of the team.

8.10.3 Automated builds

Continuous integration cannot be performed without automated testing and build tools, because it is continuous and the overhead of continuous testing cannot be performed manually. Build automation is the creation of scripts that automatically perform developer tasks such as:

- compiling code;
- running tests;
- performing code analysis;

- assembling code components into features (also known as 'build');
- deploying to environments;
- creating system documentation.

Agile deliveries should have the ability to run automated build continuously and therefore deploy continuously. In the event of a broken build, priority should be given to fix the build so that the team can continue their work with confidence. If a build has been successful, it is then possible to automate the deployment to a test environment and run the automated continuous integration tests. Automated builds should be scheduled to run on a regular frequency, at least daily.

8.10.4 Code review and peer review

Whilst automated builds are a good way to automatically check many aspects of software, they cannot detect everything. Humans are arguably much better than machines at checking that code is well written, designed and maintainable. There are a number of different ways to approach this: two common Agile approaches are that either a developer can submit completed code (for example) for peer review before committing the code, or the XP practice of pair programming can be adopted (see Section 14.1).

Peer reviews are performed with people of a similar level of experience to the person that created the product to be reviewed. The key is that peer reviews must not slow down the Agile process; therefore they may only be focused on key products or may be implemented more as a sample test intermittently. As usual in Agile, common sense should prevail and the amount and rigour of code review should be implemented in line with the complexity and rigour of the product required.

PART 3
APPLYING AGILE PRINCIPLES

9 INDIVIDUALS AND INTERACTIONS OVER PROCESSES AND TOOLS

This chapter of our book will discuss the importance of motivated human beings, and the interaction between them, to enable effective Agile delivery. We will look at what motivates individuals and present some ideas to help motivate individuals and teams. We will overview some ideas for enabling self-organising teams and discuss their importance to Agile emergent design. We will also look at the importance of understanding team dynamics and how to enable dynamic delivery within a team.

The Agile lead is the person who is responsible for facilitating processes and enabling individuals and the team to be as effective as they can be. This does not mean that the Agile lead needs to be an expert psychologist, however, an appreciation of team building and what enables individuals and interactions to be effective is important.

9.1 MOTIVATED AND TALENTED INDIVIDUALS

The fifth of the twelve principles underlying the Agile Manifesto (see Section 1.2) starts with 'Build projects around motivated individuals...'

Motivation releases energy and creativity and is an essential component of high performance. The following sections will look at a few different approaches to understanding what motivates individuals and the vital role that talent plays in achieving high performance.

9.1.1 Hierarchy of needs

Maslow noted:

> It is quite true that man lives by bread alone – when there is no bread. But what happens to man's desires when there is plenty of bread and when his belly is chronically filled?
>
> (Maslow, 1943)

Maslow's approach towards developing a humanistic psychological model related to change deviated from the common path that earlier psychologists followed (analysing people as a 'bag of symptoms'). His starting point was to identify the factors that contribute to creativity, compassion, spontaneity, morality and problem solving. Through observations of subjects that exhibited characteristics of meta-motivation, the urge for continuous improvement and achievement, Maslow developed the 'hierarchy of needs' (see Figure 9.1).

Figure 9.1 Maslow's hierarchy of needs

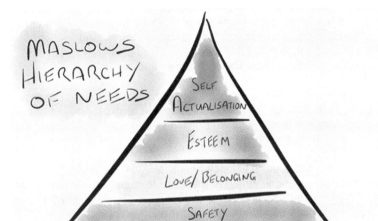

Maslow suggested that, once our basic needs are met, our behaviour will be driven by meeting higher-level needs. He suggested that there is a hierarchy of needs and once the needs lower down the hierarchy are met, further needs come into focus.

These different levels of needs are often expressed as a pyramid, originally with five layers, later expanded to eight, (Maslow,1970a,b; Figure 9.1).

The cornerstone of Maslow's theory was the assumption that human beings have inner impetus to continually develop and succeed. He assumed that human beings have the natural propensity to move towards self-actualisation by satisfying preceding needs. For instance, individuals will not focus their attention on self-actualisation if physiological needs have not been satisfied adequately.

The first four layers of the pyramid, called deficiency needs, are perceived as fundamental to one's wellbeing: physical needs, safety, love and friendship, and self-esteem. Need deficiency is considered a great motivator, as absence of satisfaction drives for further achievement.

Human survival requirements, such as food, water and air, comprise physiological needs. Sexual release and reproduction also belong in this category. The absence of these will create various psychological symptoms, such as hunger, thirst, discomfort and frustration.

The next group of needs that takes precedence once physiological needs are satisfied adequately is safety needs. They are concerned with physical safety, economic security, health and wellbeing, and protection against accidents/illness.

With safety needs fulfilled, love and belonging become prominent and dominate behaviour. These interpersonal needs are related to affection and involvement from an emotional perspective, and therefore require a degree of reciprocity. The sense of belonging and acceptance, for instance in working groups, church congregations, professional bodies and sports teams, can foster creativity and motivation. Although higher in the pyramid, it is perceived of particular significance, as loneliness and neglect may lead to social anxiety, withdrawal and depression.

The penultimate group in Maslow's hierarchy covers self-esteem and self-respect, which can be fulfilled through achieving competence or excellence in particular skills at professional, personal and social levels. These provide the sense of contribution, achievement, recognition, freedom and attention.

In spite of adequately fulfilling deficiency needs, Maslow observed the continual need to discover one's full potential, which is the need for self-actualisation: 'the desire to accomplish everything that one is capable of becoming'. Once individuals have achieved self-actualisation they can provide their support to others.

Subsequent research has confirmed that these **needs** are indeed universal (although there is actually no evidence that the specific **hierarchy** is similarly universal (Wahba and Bridwell, 1976). As such, Maslow's model can help identify what motivates people depending on which needs they are trying to meet.

Maslow's work is also a foundation of many motivational theories, one of which is described in Section 9.1.3.

9.1.2 Management's attitude determines motivation

Douglas McGregor's seminal 1960 work *The Human Side of Enterprise* (McGregor, 1960; McGregor and Gershenfeld, 2006) proposed that the interaction between management and employees is the primary source of motivation at work. McGregor drew out two possible sets of beliefs managers might hold, which he labelled Theory X and Theory Y (Table 9.1).

Theory X sees employees as inherently lazy and genuinely disliking work. It assumes that they require close supervision and control systems; show lack of ambition without an appealing incentive programme; avoid taking responsibility; operate under punishment and threats; and that their personal goals go against organisational goals and their creativity and imagination are not used at work.

In contrast, Theory Y assumes that employees are ambitious, self-motivated and self-controlled; treat work as natural and normal; take initiative for their own learning; accept responsibility and commit to organisation's objectives; and that they appreciate and respond positively to recognition and encouragement, enjoy problem solving activities and feel demotivated if their talents are not fully used.

According to McGregor, a Theory X manager will focus on methods of control and punishment to drive productivity. In contrast a Theory Y manager will focus on creating the right conditions for the employees to be largely self-directed.

Table 9.1 McGregor's Theory X and Theory Y

Theory X managers believe that employees...	Theory Y managers believe that, given the right conditions, employees...
Hate work	Like and need work
Seek money and security	Seek to be involved and realise their potential
Have to be forced to work	Drive themselves and work effectively
Prefer to be told what to do	Take initiative
Are rarely creative	Are naturally highly creative
Are selfish	Commit themselves to larger goals

Whether employees display Theory X or Theory Y behaviour is a consequence of how management treat them. This means that generally managers will get what they expect – if they expect and manage for Theory X behaviour, they will typically get employees displaying Theory X behaviour.

McGregor also notes that Theory Y behaviour leads to better outcomes for an organisation as it typically results in greater productivity. This holds particularly true for large organisations undertaking complex work. This concept is strongly related to Schneider's culture change model (see Section 3.2) – Theory 'Y' managers enable transformation to Agile, whereas theory 'X' managers block Agile.

An Agile leadership style should be in alignment with McGregor's Theory Y, which views employees in a positive light. As in Agile, that puts individuals and teams first, McGregor's research outcomes prove that teams under Theory Y management showed better performance in comparison to Theory X teams.

9.1.3 Some factors only demotivate

In another classic study on motivation, this time in 1968, a researcher named Herzberg proposed a refinement to Maslow's and an addition to McGregor's approach (Herzberg, 1968). He investigated the determining factors that influence employee motivation and performance. The research outcomes divided the factors found into two distinct categories:

- hygiene factors – which do not contribute to job satisfaction, although their absence may have detrimental results; and

- motivators – which give positive satisfaction.

Hygiene factors comprise: pay, company policy, quality of supervision/management, working relations, working conditions, status and security. Motivators comprise: achievement, recognition, responsibility, advancement, learning, type and nature of work.

He found that a number of the things people often think of as motivational don't in fact motivate at all. For example, Herzberg discovered that increasing salary, status, job security and so on do not necessarily increase people's satisfaction with their work – they do not energise them and leave them smiling at the end of a long day. This does not mean that people are indifferent to these things – but they are hygiene factors rather than motivational factors. This means that not having them in a quantity that is perceived as fair will lead to dissatisfaction and demotivation. However, increases beyond this minimum requirement have no effect on people's motivation.

On the other hand, Herzberg found that there are factors that do lead to higher motivation; in particular making the work itself more challenging and meaningful, recognising people for doing a great job and giving people the ability to grow their skills and experience.

9.1.4 Motivation comes from autonomy, mastery and purpose

More recently in 2010, Daniel Pink expanded on McGregor's work and looked at the conditions required for employees to adopt Theory Y behaviour and achieve higher levels of performance (Pink, 2009).

He suggested that work patterns were changing and there were fewer and fewer jobs that could be managed with what he refers to as the 'carrot-and-stick' approach (Theory X). Harnessing the intrinsic motivations of employees ('self-actualisation' in Maslow's hierarchy) therefore becomes a significant competitive advantage for companies.

Examples of recent success based on harnessing intrinsic motivation include Wikipedia, the Open Source software movement and the growth in businesses with a social mission.

Pink summarises the factors that need to be present to release high levels of motivation and drive as autonomy, mastery and purpose.

- **Autonomy** – people's desire to direct their own lives and to gain control over some (or all) of the four main aspects of work: what, how, when and with whom.

- **Mastery** – becoming better at something that matters to an individual. This can be achieved by taking on tasks that allow people to develop skills further. Mastery is fostered by an environment where learning is encouraged and mistakes are tolerated.

- **Purpose** – fulfilling a natural desire in people to contribute to a cause greater than themselves.

9.1.5 Talent comes from purposeful practice

To achieve high performance, motivation needs to be coupled with **talent**. So where does talent come from? Are people born with it or can they acquire it? Matthew Syed argues for the latter, and states that (Syed, 2011):

- 10,000 hours of practice is a minimum to become 'talented' (= 2.7 hours a day for 10 years). While people are attracted to stories of child prodigies or the effortless genius, Syed claims that talented individuals invariably always got a unique opportunity to put in a lot of practice very early on in life. Mozart, for example, who composed his first true masterpiece at 21, has been calculated to have put in an eye-watering 3,500 hours of music practice even before his sixth birthday.

- Practice needs to be purposeful. Not all practice is useful. People only develop when they repeatedly try things that are just out of reach and get quality feedback on their performance. The paradox of excellence is that it is built on necessary failure. The learning process is often best facilitated by an expert coach. For example, whilst Mozart's father was only so-so as a musician, he was highly accomplished as a teacher. His book on violin instruction published the year Mozart was born remained influential for decades.

Laslo Polgar (1989) provides perhaps the most amazing and audacious demonstration of the effects of purposeful practice. A Hungarian educational psychologist and early advocate of the practice theory of talent, he set out to show that by purposeful practice, his three daughters could become world-class in a chosen area.

He selected chess as, unlike art or music, chess provides an objective rating for a player, which meant that the results of the demonstration would be clear. Also, he himself had no particular background in chess. The results were clear indeed. Laslo's three daughters are:

- **Susan** First ever female Grandmaster.
- **Sofia** International Master.
- **Judit** Youngest ever Grandmaster, considered greatest female chess player of all time.

Engaging in purposeful practice leads to high performance – and the opposite is also true. Experiments by Dweck (2012) suggest that treating people as being innately talented (i.e. considering talent as something they are born with) disempowers them to the extent that there is a drop in performance. This is because they act in fear of being 'found out' that they are not as talented as expected.

9.2 EMERGENT DESIGN FROM SELF-ORGANISING TEAMS

The eleventh of the twelve principles underlying the Agile Manifesto is 'The best architectures, requirements, and designs emerge from self-organising teams.' This section discusses what 'emergent design' means, why it is so important and why self-organising teams are vital to the concept of emergent design.

9.2.1 'Emergent design' – why is it important?

Agile teams aim to unrestrict business and technical opportunities by not designing everything up front; instead design is based on facts that are learned whilst developing stories. The fundamental design thinking that is in place is driven by the concept of 'last responsible moment' (a concept from Lean; Liker, 2004). The 'last responsible moment' is the moment at which something needs to happen, for example a design decision needs to be made.

This ties in with the concept of 'real options' (Matts, 2007), which means keeping your options open for as long as you possibly can and making a decision when you are in the best position to make it with confidence.

An example might be having to put out an order for a piece of hardware, which has a certain lead time on it. The last responsible moment is governed by that lead time, and we have to find out enough about the hardware to make the order by that time. This means we need to do enough experimentation and development to gather the required knowledge by the time the last responsible moment comes, so that we make the right decision. We might even find that at the last responsible moment we don't actually need it anyway.

It may appear attractive to make all design decisions up front, commonly known as big design up front (BDUF). However, there are two main advantages to implementing the last responsible moment when making design decisions:

- If all design decisions are made up front, any changes may cause significant implementation effort. This will restrict opportunities to change and improve the design as the product is being developed. If design decisions are made at the last responsible moment, it means design opportunities can be implemented as they arise. This is commonly known as 'opportunistic design', and is a key enabler to allow businesses to be flexible.

- If teams wait until the last responsible moment to make design decisions, they can make decisions based on evidence that is identified as the system is being built. This typically means that decisions are of a higher quality, because they are not just theoretical decisions based on little evidence.

Therefore, in an Agile product delivery, teams do not implement BDUF, they implement EDUF (enough design up front). How much design is 'enough' design depends on the dynamism of the environment in which the product is being built, the experience of the team, and many other factors. What is essential is that somebody in the team understands enough about the technical design risks associated with what is being built to make decisions on what elements of the design it is safe to develop, and what elements of the design need to be defined up front.

What defines EDUF largely depends on the complexity and size of the Agile delivery. If Agile is applied across a programme or project that is larger than a couple of teams, then the project will need to ensure that all the teams align to a single design and architecture that can be integrated. Therefore medium to large Agile deliveries may need some high-level design architecture principles and enough design up front to enable the teams to design their services and components in a way that is flexible but enables integration.

More information on technical excellence and good design within Agile is available at Section 10.4.

9.2.2 Self-organising teams and emergent design

As discussed in Section 6.2.2, self-organising teams are empowered, within agreed boundaries, to deliver fit-for-purpose products, in a fit-for-purpose way, within the most effective timescale.

Typically what happens within a self-organising team in relation to emergent design is that there will be some overarching design principles that teams must or should align to. However, whenever detailed design decisions are to be made, teams will make them, for the following reasons:

- If teams are forced to align to an externally defined detailed design they are unlikely to 'go the extra mile' to try and identify or implement any opportunities to make the design better (opportunistic design).

- It is likely that the only people who can effectively make the right detailed design decisions are team members. Nobody else will understand the evolving design as well as the team does.

9.3 TEAM DYNAMICS

To be successful, Agile teams need to develop high levels of trust and collaboration between team members, customers and stakeholders. Management will need to articulate a compelling team purpose and also be willing to transfer real power to the teams. This section looks at ways to identify team dynamics as well as dysfunction in teams to help the Agile lead to put actions in place to increase team dynamics.

9.3.1 Tuckman's theory of team evolution

Bruce Tuckman (1965) observed that teams do not function effectively as a unit all the time. Rather, teams go through different states. The state in which a team is most productive is referred to as 'performing'. Other possible states for teams are 'forming' (polite and cautious when a team is new), 'storming' (conflict comes to the surface) and 'norming' (conflict is being resolved) (see Figure 9.2).

Whilst a team will need to run through these stages to achieve a 'performing' state, there is no guarantee that it will remain there. External factors or change, such as the introduction of a new team member, may cause teams to revisit the 'storming' stage.

Figure 9.2 Tuckman's theory of team evolution

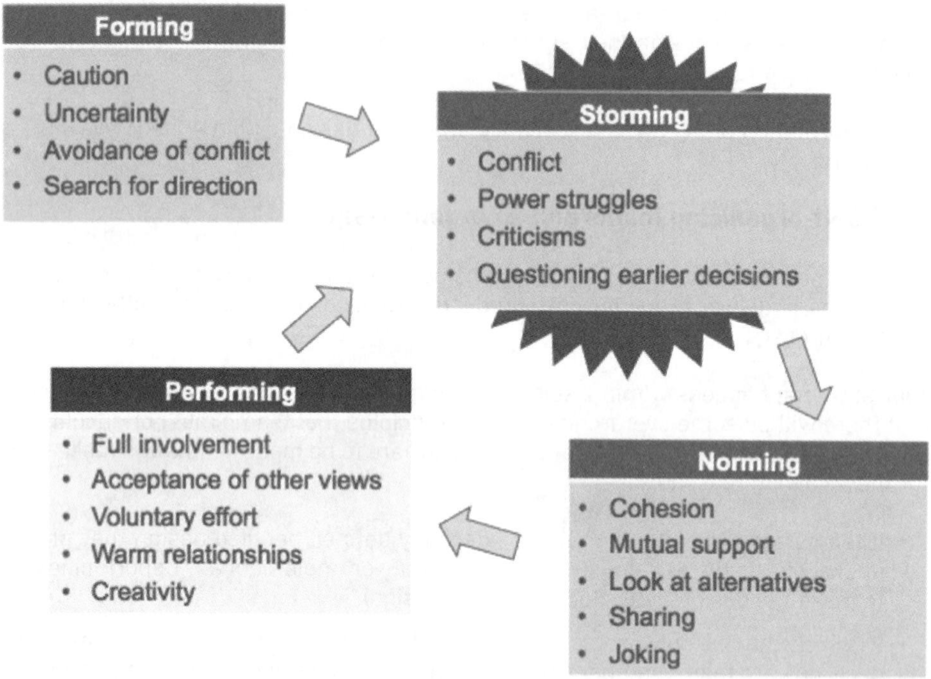

9.3.2 Lencioni – the five dysfunctions of teams

This is a model developed by Patrick Lencioni (2002; Figure 9.3). It lists five dysfunctions that prevent high performance.

The five dysfunctions are:

- **Absence of trust** – Team members need to be able to trust each other by being 'vulnerable' and admitting that everyone can make mistakes. This is where the Agile lead needs to start the process by talking about experiences they have had and actions that highlight their own weaknesses, thereby showing where they need the team's support.

- **Fear of conflict** – Often people 'fear to rock the boat' as this is indicative of a disruptive and 'non-collegiate' colleague. This creates the psychological phenomenon of 'group think'. If teams actively suppress dissenting viewpoints and isolate themselves from outside influences, then they will only have a very limited, inward-looking approach to problem solving. Therefore, it is vital to encourage debate and alternative viewpoints so that an outward thinking approach evolves.

- **Lack of commitment** – This is also sometimes referred to as 'cabinet responsibility'. Cabinet responsibility refers to the fact that, if there is a vote of no confidence passed in parliament (Westminster), the government is collectively responsible and resigns as a whole. For Agile teams, this means that, following a healthy debate in a conflict discussion, the Agile lead must identify and state a clear 'goal' and get the team's commitment to it. Any meeting where individuals leave and then go against the commitment undermines everything that the team do.

- **Avoidance of accountability** – In a team, individuals need to be held to account. This is not about assigning blame, but about committing to an outcome, meaning that a team member says to the other team members and the lead that they can get this done and will be accountable for doing so. The Agile lead is responsible for ensuring that individual members are not 'over-committing' during the process and that collectively the team gather around to support and help members who are struggling.

- **Inattention to results** – This is about the team being accountable for the overall result and the Agile lead keeping the team focused on that, rather than allowing individuals to 'showboat' their personal success. An important aspect of this is the decision on what should be measured when deciding a course of action and then sticking to that as the measureable. It is the true focus on collective accountability.

Figure 9.3 Lencioni: five team dysfunctions

Key to Lencioni's thinking is to recognise the simplicity of the pyramid. In a way we can think of the pyramid as a building construction. If you have no foundations (i.e. trust), then the house will collapse. If you have a building that is not watertight with a good roof (i.e. inattention to results), then the weather (business climate and conditions) will quickly seep into the rest of the building and destroy what you have built.

To summarise and re-frame the five dysfunctions as positives (see Figure 9.4), functional teams will:

Figure 9.4 Lencioni: a functional team

- trust their colleagues;
- hold passionate and unfiltered debate on important issues;
- commit to goals;
- hold their members accountable for commitments;
- have a collective set of results that are well understood.

10 WORKING SOFTWARE OVER COMPREHENSIVE DOCUMENTATION

10.1 SATISFY THE CUSTOMER AND CONTINUOUS DELIVERY OF VALUE

The Agile principle being discussed in this section is 'Our highest priority is to satisfy the customer through early and continuous delivery of valuable software.' We will look at the concept of continuous delivery in more detail, and how to perceive value in a context; for example, how to order the backlog focused on RoI (Return on Investment) rather than simply reductions in cost.

The sooner a product is delivered, the sooner the product starts to produce business value and the sooner business and technical feedback can be sought. Additionally and importantly, the sooner teams can inspect a product via feedback, the sooner they can adapt to deliver the appropriate stories as they evolve.

The continuous delivery of value is why Agile aims for deliveries of valuable useable features from small delivery batch sizes (iterations/sprints). Agile deliveries can be made (and sometimes can only be made) within releases, projects etc as we have discussed elsewhere in this book; however, the longer the team waits to deliver valuable features the bigger the delivery batch size with the inherent problems that causes (risk of confusion, errors, low productivity etc).

In today's world, it appears, there are largely two types of business:

- businesses that are 'IT businesses'; and
- businesses that are fundamentally reliant on IT.

Therefore if the delivery of IT-driven business value is restricted in its ability to be fast and flexible, then the business that relies on that delivery will be severely, if not potentially fatally, constrained.

10.1.1 Product flow and business value

Effective product flow, i.e. ensuring that the right products are developed as continuously, is arguably the key driver to generating value in any product development, whether it is IT or otherwise. A lot of the discussion in this section is based on thinking from Donald G Reinertsen and his book on product flow: *The principles of product development flow: second generation lean product development* (Reinertsen, 2009).

In his book Reinertsen lists eight major themes that lie at the core of flow-based product development. These are:

- **Economics** – establish an integrated economically based decision-making framework; if you only understand one thing understand the cost of delay.

- **Queues** – identify work queues and endeavour to make them as short as possible, because long queues, amongst other things, add risk and increase cycle time.

- **Variability** – within software development teams may be creating a new product, therefore variability is required. Removing variability may remove innovation. Therefore the system to be implemented must be able to deal with variability.

- **Batch size** – large batch sizes create large variability and an environment where many skills may be needed to enable delivery of a single product feature, leading to queues caused by handoffs between roles.

- **Work-in-progress constraints** – apply work-in-progress constraints to match work in progress to capacity, therefore helping to remove queues.

- **Cadence, synchronisation and flow control** – create a delivery heartbeat (cadence) within short timescales to ensure fast feedback cycles and predictability (removal of 'noise'). Synchronise across many teams on a standard, regular and short delivery cadence.

- **Fast feedback** – enables effective communication between technical teams and between technical teams and the business; this leads to more accurate products.

- **Decentralised control** – this leads to faster and more accurate decisions.

Although Agile approaches support many of Reinertsen's themes, in the following we will look at 'economics' as it is directly related to quantifying and measuring business value.

Reinertsen proposes 21 different economic principles within the 'Economics' theme. The core principle we want to discuss in this section is principle three, which looks at the 'cost of delay'. This principle is based on principles one and two:

Economic principle number one is 'the principle of quantified overall economics: select actions based on quantified overall economic impact' (Reinertsen, 2009). This principle drives the definition of value within the organisation using an overall economic framework. The intent of the framework is to manage complex multi-variable decisions by expressing all operational impacts (e.g. waste, cycle time, efficiency) in the same unit of measure – which is 'lifecycle profit impact', i.e. the impact on business profit from varying any variable.

When a business applies this principle, it enables customers and stakeholders to define an agreed ordering of the backlog based primarily on lifecycle profit impact. Therefore, lifecycle profit impact is focused on the overall value of delivery rather than just cost reduction or any other single aspect of value delivery.

Economic principle number two is the principle of interconnected dynamics, meaning that no one thing can be changed in an organisation without affecting other things. For example, the customer may want to add more stories before implementing anything. They then make the (erroneous) decision to reduce testing and refactoring to enable quick implementation of the stories. This decision may impact on the following:

- In the short term the cycle time may be decreased and therefore delivery of stories increased.
- The development cost in the short-term may decrease.
- The perceived short-term value-add may increase; however, long-term value-add may significantly decrease.
- The support and maintenance cost of the product may significantly increase as many more defects might occur later in the lifecycle when they are far more costly to fix.
- Significant technical debt may be added to the system, which will make the system very difficult and costly to enhance in the future.

The product flow solution is to create an overall interconnected project economic framework. The framework treats projects as a black box, and the focus of each project is to produce lifecycle profits. Reinertsen highlights five interconnected key measurements for the project, all of which contribute towards overall lifecycle profits. These are:

- Cycle time – work start to finish time.
- Product cost – the cost of the whole product lifecycle, from cradle to grave, i.e. the costs to manufacture the product. For pure software products arguably not that significant, although things like license costs or any other transaction costs should be included. For products that have hardware this is more significant, as it includes the costs of the parts and labour to put it together.
- Product value – the revenue the product generates over its lifetime. It is important to have this especially when considering cost of delay as delivering late can have a negative effect on revenue if a market opportunity is missed.
- Development expense – the development costs of the product.
- Risk – a quantification of the level of risk an organisation is willing to take on various parts of the development. It involves using probability of achieving a certain level of revenue balanced against what it costs to produce it.

If a team can ascertain the lifecycle profits of stories, they can then ascertain the value of each story and therefore the relative cost of delaying any story, or indeed bringing forward higher-value stories.

Economic principle number three is 'the principle of quantified cost of delay: if you only quantify one thing, quantify the cost of delay' (Reinertsen, 2009). The cost of delay is the cost of something being delayed on the profitability of the business.

If all variables under one single unit – defined as lifecycle profit impact – can be brought together and the interconnectivity between decisions using this unit be visualised, the cost of delay can be quantified.

Quantifying the cost of delay enables the customer to identify the relative cost of stories being available now, sooner or later. Quantifying cost of delay in lifecycle profit impact enables all collaboration and conversations about relative ordering and priority to be moved away from simplistic cost-cutting and moved towards business value conversations.

Within an Agile team the ability to exactly quantify the cost of delay is less important as the exact mathematics is not the essential aim; instead, the ability to visualise the relative cost of delay across stories within the backlog is vital to the customer being able to order the backlog effectively.

10.1.2 The product flow economic model and prioritisation

A relatively common mistake made by Agile teams is to qualify the ordering of stories in the backlog from the perspective of a single economic variable (although Reinertsen does suggest that if only one thing is measured – which it shouldn't be – it should be cost of delay).

For example, if the team is too technically focused, there is a risk that the only variable being considered is development cost, and therefore there is insufficient focus on whether (or not) value is actually being added to the business.

Another example is when the customer orders activity based only on business value and does not take into account development cost. In this situation lots of stories may be delivered, but because development cost and sensible sequencing of development resources has not been taken into account, the cost and timescale of developing the product may be significantly larger than necessary.

The sequencing of the backlog needs to take into account the overall economic model, and the related variables. Once the cost of delay of a particular story in a particular backlog has been ascertained, the customer can then think about how to sequence the backlog by using the product flow model. When considering cost of delay, the following economic approaches can be applied to ordering a backlog:

FIFO: First in First Out. The first feature that comes into the backlog is the next feature that is delivered. This may be an appropriate way to manage an incidents backlog where all the incidents are of the same importance, however, it will not be appropriate for many product developments.

SJF: Shortest Job First. If the cost of delay is equal across stories, then order the stories with the least duration first.

HCDF: High Cost of Delay First. If the cost of delay is not equal but the duration to deliver the feature is equal, then order the feature with the highest cost of delay first.

WSJF: Weighted Shortest Job First. Where nothing is equal, do the weighted shortest job first. The weighted shortest job = cost of delay/duration

10.2 DELIVER WORKING SOFTWARE FREQUENTLY

The Agile principle described in this section is 'Deliver working software frequently, from a couple of weeks to a couple of months, with a preference to the shorter timescale.'

So what exactly is meant by 'working software'? Essentially, 'working software' is when the software is 'done' (see Section 10.2.1). The ultimate aim is that working, 'done' software is always delivered to the live environment where the customer gains benefits.

There are numerous benefits of frequently delivering working software.

- **Regular delivery cadence** Most Agile frameworks recommend that a regular delivery heartbeat or cadence of the same length is implemented. This cadence is associated with sprints/iterations (typically every 2 to 4 weeks), and/or releases, which contain multiple sprints/iterations of typically every 1 to 3 months. Setting a continuous sprint/iteration cadence enables teams to focus on delivering in a regular time frame and allows stakeholders to make themselves available at regular points to review what is being created by the team. A regular short delivery cadence enables more frequent feedback from the stakeholders; also, the team are much less likely to experience 'noise' (unplanned interruptions during iterations) that could seriously affect the team's delivery capability.

- **Commitment and trust** It is next to impossible to implement Agile successfully if teams continually miss their iteration/sprint goals. Many Agile frameworks value commitment against a clearly stated iteration/sprint goal, and an environment of trust cannot be built if the team continually fail to deliver against those commitments.

  A common cause of delivery failure is that working product is not delivered frequently enough. A team's delivery focus can be lost easily if teams cannot see an achievable goal within a timescale that they are able to commit to, or alternatively it might be that the goal as originally agreed keeps changing.

- **Understanding** A common cause of misalignment between business stake-holders and technical teams is that they do not understand each other. This can be exacerbated if delivery is being driven from detailed specification documents, as it is unlikely that both parties will interpret the document in the same way. The frequent delivery of working software ensures that the customer and stakeholders have full visibility and so understand what is being delivered.

- **Enabling 'Lean start-up'** (see Section 14.7) The most effective way to validate the market-fitness of a product is when the actual end users interact with the working product. Regular releases of new functionality allow the end user to try out the evolving product and feedback instantly.

- **Continuous improvement** Delivering frequently allows the team to regularly reflect upon their work and adapt the delivery processes as required.

- **Reduced business risk** Short feedback cycles are essential for a successful product delivery. If interactions between teams and key stakeholders are rare it is highly likely that the wrong product will be built. When working software is delivered regularly, the business risks and associated costs are significantly reduced as this means that via inspection of the product the customer can ensure the business case is being achieved and is still robust.

There is a philosophy in Agile called 'fail fast', meaning that if the requirements of the business case are not met, the delivery can fail fast before too much time and money is wasted. Many Agile experts see this really as 'learn fast'. The team, customer and stakeholders learn fast that they are going in the wrong direction and therefore stop before deciding which is the right direction to go in, or whether to re-start at all.

- **Reduce technical risk** By regularly releasing increments to a product the change to the product between versions is smaller. This reduces the technical risk to the business and makes implementation easier. It also means that any appropriate corrective actions can be implemented effectively, frequently and with confidence.

Product delivery every few weeks may not be practical or required within a large complex integrated systems development. In this scenario it may only be feasible to deliver integrated working software produced by multiple teams within releases of multiple iterations/sprints.

10.2.1 Definition of 'done'

The 'definition of done' (DoD) refers to the point at which the product is fit for purpose and the customer will sign it off. DoDs can be related to sprint, release and project goals.

Most teams create DoD lists that define what must be signed off before a product is at 'done' status. This may be something as simple as 'code complete' and 'tests complete' though usually it is a list that will contain items such as:

- Story done (acceptance criteria met).
- Standards and guidelines done. There are certain requirements that relate to everything being produced (such as performance, scalability, auditability etc.). Therefore it makes sense to define requirements that apply to every story as standards or guidelines.
- Code done.
- Code review done.
- Unit, integration, system UA tests done.
- Deploy to environment done.
- Documentation done.
- Refactoring done.

10.3 WORKING SOFTWARE AS A MEASURE OF PROGRESS

This section relates to the Agile Manifesto principle 'Working software is the primary measure of progress.'

In a traditional non-Agile environment milestones are typically set against the stages of whatever delivery approach is being used. For example, in a Waterfall delivery, typical milestones will be aligned to the stages in the Waterfall process: analysis, design, build, test, implement. Associated with those milestones will be Waterfall documents, for example, requirements specifications and functional specifications.

In an Agile delivery, progress is considered to have been made when the value-added product is delivered to the live environment for the customer, thereby adding value to the customer's business. This does not necessarily mean that delivery of value-add software is the only measure of progress (others might include defect rates or the amount of technical debt and so on), but it is certainly the core measurement.

Agile audits tend to be performed against outcomes delivered by value-added software, rather than against documents or milestones.

A significant benefit of using working systems as the primary measure of progress is that it focuses the Agile team on working in an integrated, collaborative way, as the only way they can deliver working software is as a team collaborating with the customer and stakeholders. In situations where the focus is on delivering documents or milestones associated with job types (e.g. an analyst delivering analytical products within an analysis stage) the team can become disjointed and a blame culture develops.

10.4 TECHNICAL EXCELLENCE AND GOOD DESIGN

This section discusses the Agile Manifesto principle 'Continuous attention to technical excellence and good design enhances agility.'

As discussed before, in an Agile delivery the customer prioritises stories to ensure the right product for the emergent business need is developed. At the same time it is also important for teams to verify that they are developing the product in the right way (the development process).

Quality is at the core of Agile product development (see Section 8.9), and a successful Agile delivery is dependent on Agile teams paying close attention to technical excellence and good design. If a feature of the product is identified as being of sub-standard design the team should make sure that a story is raised to specifically address the concern.

If teams do not maintain appropriate technical excellence and good design throughout the development process, it will become increasingly difficult to add further product increments as the product will get unnecessarily complex, therefore decreasing the value-add. It is too easy for the team to continue to add stories to a product without considering the overall integrated technical design of the product, and in most cases this will lead to a product that is fragile and unmaintainable.

Lack of focus on technical excellence and good design also creates great difficulties for the delivery to be Agile at all as significant time is spent dealing with the problems caused by high technical debt.

10.4.1 Technical debt

Allowing inappropriate design or architecture leads to what Agile calls 'technical debt'. Technical debt creates systems that are extremely expensive to support and maintain as they are badly designed, badly documented and typically full of defects (see Figure 10.1 - shows that technical debt pushes problems later in the delivery lifecycle where they are significantly more expensive to fix). It will also make the system very difficult to enhance, thereby restricting the ability to deliver stories frequently and add value to the business.

Figure 10.1 Relative cost for phase that a defect is fixed

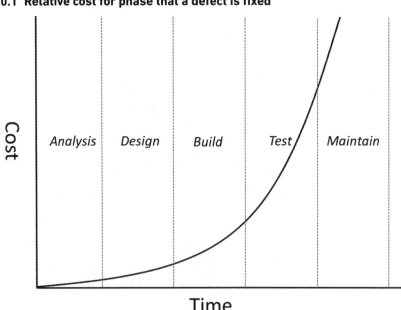

Technical debt, like financial debt, accrues compound interest. For example, if teams perform a quick fix once, the next time there is a problem, they are highly likely to implement a quick fix again. This approach usually does not address underlying problems, and the effect of these problems is compounded as the product is developed further, leading to technical debt. Once technical debt has been allowed into a system it can grow very quickly and become a core design feature/problem of the system. Technical debt can be addressed through refactoring (see Section 8.10.1).

10.4.2 Architecture and design frameworks

Agile does not mandate the usage of any specific design or architecture framework, and it is outside the boundaries of this book to discuss these in detail. Agile teams may (or may not) get benefit from using architecture principles such as SOA (Service Orientated Architectures), architecture approaches such as TOGAF (The Open Group Architecture Framework) or design approaches such as UML (Unified Modelling Language).

However, when implementing any architecture or design framework it is essential to also consider another core Agile principle: Simplicity, the art of maximising the amount of work not done (see Chapter 13). It can be very easy for a team to deliver everything defined within a particular architecture or design framework without thinking specifically about which artefacts from the framework demonstrably add value. It is the responsibility of the Agile lead to coach the team to think about simplicity and to only use those aspects of a framework that demonstrably add value.

11 CUSTOMER COLLABORATION OVER CONTRACT NEGOTIATIONS

11.1 BUSINESS PEOPLE AND DEVELOPERS MUST WORK TOGETHER

This section discusses the Agile principle 'Business people and developers must work together daily throughout the project.'

In today's complex knowledge-based IT-driven world, no single delivery discipline (e.g. analyst, coder, designer) can be successful working on their own. To achieve successful product delivery, collaboration is essential.

Collaboration delivers the following benefits:

- Teams can understand the evolving vision of the business, allowing them to continually assess whether the goal of a time-box is still aligned to the business need and is still deliverable within the time-box.

- The customer can effectively communicate the evolving team approach back to the rest of the business. The resulting trust relationship between the business and the team is a huge enabler for collaborative Agile delivery. If ongoing communication is not maintained between the team and the business, or the team does not deliver value to the business continuously, it is likely to lead to concerns about delivery and possibly even micromanagement. This can cause interruptions (noise) that may significantly reduce the productivity of the team or even fundamentally derail the delivery.

- Business people and the team can agree on an accurate solution to problems. This collaboration must be continuous (at least daily) rather than being limited to infrequent occasions such as planning sessions.

- Business people can answer team questions as they arise and vice versa. Business people tend to have a vast amount of knowledge of the required business system that the product supports, while the team are experts in the technologies available to develop and implement products. This interchange increases the effectiveness of the knowledge discovery process, shortens feedback loops and dramatically reduces the likelihood of delivering the wrong functionality due to misinterpretation of requirements and so increases efficiency.

- As the customer signs off individual stories as 'done' as they become available, they need to interact with the team throughout the delivery time-box. This enables everyone to effectively track progress based on actual delivery of working software within the time-box, with the inherent associated benefits.

11.2 REFLECT AND ADJUST (INSPECT AND ADAPT) REGULARLY

This section discusses the Agile principle 'At regular intervals, the team reflects on how to become more effective, then tunes and adjusts its behaviour accordingly.'

The three foundations of Agile as an empirical process are inspection, adaptation and transparency (see Section 2.6). The inspection and adaptation cycle allows for an accurate product to be delivered within a time-box; it also helps to define and evolve team processes and the continual improvement (Kaizen) that a team implements.

In more traditional delivery approaches there is sometimes a 'lessons learned' process at the end of a release or at the end of a project. In contrast, the majority of Agile frameworks include regular reflection and adjustment points during the ongoing delivery of the product. These reflection and adjustment points can occur at the end of a time-box, or within the time-box. Wherever they are placed they must be regular, with regular meaning at the least at the boundaries of every sprint/iteration time-box (every 2 to 4 weeks).

12 RESPONDING TO CHANGE OVER FOLLOWING A PLAN

12.1 EMBRACE CHANGE

In this section we will look at how change can be embraced in an Agile environment and describe a few change management models that are useful in supporting change on an organisational level.

12.1.1 Embracing change whilst delivering a product

It was Heraclitus who said 'The only thing that is constant is change'; this is particularly true in complicated and complex environments. Therefore, in Agile deliveries, teams need to adopt practices that enable a knowledge–discovery process and allow them to take corrective action as they identify detailed requirements and technology needs.

This means that teams need to embrace change and make it a core part of the process rather than see it as an external source that needs to be resisted – basically they need to 'be Agile' and have an understanding of why they should embrace the principles described in this book, most specifically the following:

- Implementing the Agile mind-set (see Section 2.1).
- Understanding environments and their suitability for Agile (see Section 2.2).
- How to work in uncertain and volatile environments (see Section 2.5).
- How the Agile process supports change (see Chapter 5).
- How the Agile roles support change (see Chapter 6).
- Stories and continuous backlog refinement enable continuous change (see Section 7.1).
- Customer collaboration is key to effectively embracing the right changes (see Section 11.1).
- MSCW prioritisation enables focus on the most important changes (see Section 7.1.4).
- Short feedback loops allow for changes to be identified and implemented effectively (see Section 8.1).
- Documentation emerges as change occurs (see Section 8.6).
- Monitoring change through daily stand-ups (see Section 8.3), show and tells (see Section 8.4), retrospectives (see Section 8.5) and visual boards (see Section 8.7).

- Design emerges as the understanding of the product evolves (see Section 9.2).
- Agile plans change as the understanding of the product evolves (see Section 7.3).
- Change should occur at a sustainable pace (see Section 8.8).

12.1.2 Embracing change organisationally

There are a number of change models that can help Agile team leads and organisations as a whole to think about behaviours that enable change to be welcomed rather than feared, and that are effective in initiating and driving a transformation to Agile.

12.1.2.1 The 11 paradoxes of leadership

Agile operates within variable environments, which requires leaders to embrace mechanisms and approaches to continuously drive change. Modern leadership is a balancing act between contradictory elements: managers should focus on short- and long-term goals, take into consideration global and local issues, inspire teamwork yet encourage individual accountability and promote their vision while following a pragmatic path.

The 11 Paradoxes of Leadership, which were defined by Dr Paul Evans at Lego (Evans, 2000), propose that modern change leaders should ideally have the following management and leadership skills:

1. To be able to build a close relationship with one's staff, and to keep a suitable distance.
2. To be able to lead, and to hold oneself in the background.
3. To trust one's staff, and to keep an eye on what is happening.
4. To be tolerant, and to know how you want things to function.
5. To keep the goals of one's department in mind, and at the same time to be loyal to the whole firm.
6. To do a good job of planning your own time, and to be flexible with your schedule.
7. To freely express your view, and to be diplomatic.
8. To be a visionary, and to keep one's feet on the ground.
9. To try to win consensus, and to be able to cut through.
10. To be dynamic, and to be reflective.
11. To be sure of yourself, and to be humble.

In an Agile environment, the Agile lead is the person who needs to consider a variety of often contradictory perspectives to manage change successfully, so an understanding of the 11 paradoxes is a useful checklist. They also provide a good reference list for the Agile team lead to highlight Agile-enabling behaviours for leaders in the organisation.

12.1.2.2 Kotter's eight-step model

Kotter's (1996) eight-step model is about enabling organisations to react successfully to opportunities, understanding the drivers behind change, and strengthening information flow across the organisation.

- **Establish a sense of urgency** This significant stage is often overlooked by change leaders. Through effective and bi-directional communication, leaders should outline the challenges in today's competition landscape, provide potential future scenarios, and understand the current state of their organisation:

  - complacency: failure to react to signs that action must be taken;
  - false urgency: focus on action that does not contribute to the desired goal;
  - true urgency: focus on action that adds value. Urgency should be driven by the belief that the macro-environment contains great opportunities, yet great hazards as well.

- **Form a powerful guiding coalition** Developing the right vision, disseminating the appropriate messages across the organisation, mitigating risk and shifting the organisational culture to new levels requires close collaboration, significant levels of trust and common goals amongst members of a power group. The formed coalition should:

  - be in a position of power to avoid impediments;
  - have expertise to make informed decisions;
  - have sufficient credibility to be accepted by the workforce;
  - be proven leaders to successfully drive change.

- **Create a new vision** Creating a clear vision facilitates the change process. A successful vision should reflect the following six qualities:

  - imaginable;
  - desirable;
  - feasible;
  - focused;
  - flexible;
  - communicable.

  In addition, a vision and its underlying strategies contribute to three significant purposes:

  - influences the nature of numerous decisions at lower levels in an organisational hierarchy;
  - creates a suitable environment and motivates employees to take action in line with the specified vision;
  - facilitates the coordination between various groups of people.

- **Communicate the vision** To minimise ambiguity, under-commitment and inconsistencies, change leaders should communicate the vision, underlying strategies and new behaviours across multiple communication channels and to the entire organisation. Kotter emphasises the importance of engaging dialogues, sessions and workshops between visionary leaders, senior management and the rest of the organisation. Communication about the transformation should follow four simple rules; it should be:

- simple;
- vivid;
- repeatable;
- invitational.

- **Empower others to act on the vision** Internal structures, resource defragmentation and impeding procedures can inhibit transformation incentives to progress sufficiently. These barriers should be removed promptly to allow empowered individuals to experiment. In addition, special attention should be paid to narrow-minded middle management, whose personal agenda may be in direct conflict with the transformation goals.

- **Plan for and create short-term wins** Low-hanging fruits, short-term visible improvements and quick wins are encouraged during the first stages of a change initiative. The guiding coalition should identify and promote these quick wins in a visible and unambiguous manner. Through vivid communication, such success proves that personal sacrifices, difficulties and struggles caused by the transformation are paying off.

- **Consolidate improvement and produce still more change** Fighting resistance during both early and mature stages of the change process should be one of the primary concerns. Even after declared victories, those who resist the change may withdraw, reappearing unexpectedly at a later stage. To avoid losing positive momentum, leadership is invaluable during this stage: recognising and rewarding individuals and teams that work towards the vision should be strongly considered.

- **Institutionalise new approaches** Regressing towards old behaviours, practices and processes should be expected, in particular if new practices have not been routed effectively in the new organisational culture. To sustain the change, the majority of the organisation should be convinced that the new status quo is superior to the old one. Change leadership should ensure that embracing the new approaches will benefit the organisation in its entirety.

12.1.2.3 J-curve change model

Throughout change initiatives, organisations exhibit particular behaviour patterns, which can be categorised in five stages, based on the J-curve change model:

1. plateau;
2. cliff;
3. valley;
4. ascent;
5. mountaintop.

During the **plateau** stage, business operations follow common patterns without any disruptions. After the introduction of a change initiative, the organisation goes through the **cliff** stage, feeling anxious and stressed due to the unknown future. At this point, leadership should provide assurances that the change initiative is heading towards the right direction and that discomfort because of change is expected.

In the **valley** stage, productivity drops significantly, as employees feel demotivated. Frustration reaches peak levels, in alignment with lack of confidence towards the new processes and behaviours. It is considered typical that employees denounce the change similar to 'this is never going to work'. The dip, also known as the **valley of death** (VoD), should be treated with extra care, as mismanagement may have a cascading effect to the rest of the organisation. As the organisation starts realising the positive outcomes from the change initiative, leadership should communicate the added value and benefits across the board.

During the **ascent** stage, change agents and other contributors should be recognised for their services of fighting against resistance and implementing the change. This will give a clear sign of approval, which will minimise any regression to the previous status quo, processes and behaviours.

The final stage, **mountaintop**, celebrates a new environment of improvement, with productivity and performance at higher levels in comparison to the plateau. This incremental change will motivate employees to keep changing their operations to achieve better results.

In an Agile environment, change leaders embrace the concepts behind the J-curve change model in order to introduce change. Frequently, change strategies are split into more manageable change initiatives, which will introduce less disruption at the team and organisational level. By sequencing such change initiatives, the final outcome is multiple J-curves following one another.

13 SIMPLICITY
The art of maximising the amount of work not done

This chapter looks at 'maximising the amount of work not done' – the tenth Agile principle. Most people interpret this principle in one of two ways. They assume this means one of the following:

1. Focusing on ensuring that only the simplest, leanest and fit-for-purpose product is delivered, especially when considering lifecycle-driven documentation, and only producing what adds value.
2. Focusing on maximising the amount of work not done when creating the product, i.e., focusing on simplicity of delivery.

Both of these interpretations are correct, so in the following we will look at both.

13.1 FIT-FOR-PURPOSE PRODUCTS

This principle has links to subjects such as time management and prioritisation and focuses on producing the simplest product that is appropriate for what the customer wants. This requires a clear business case for all stories that are delivered. This principle is therefore about reducing clutter and keeping the backlog focused on whatever needs to be delivered first (see Section 7.1).

Steven Covey (1989) refers to this concept as his Habit 3 or 'Put the First things First'. We can see how this is also represented in the Pareto Principle (originated by Koch, 1998), i.e. that 80 per cent of the value/functionality/benefit comes from 20 per cent of the effort put in.

The idea of simplicity in information systems has been both supported and challenged. The most quoted source within the Agile community in favour of simplicity is the Standish Group's series of reports on IT entitled 'The chaos report' (Standish, 2002). The overall summary provided by the 2002 chaos report is clear – when the focus strays from producing fit-for-purpose systems, the analytical evidence shows that people simply don't use a significant majority of the features that are developed.

The following figures were presented at the 'XP2002' conference by Jim Johnson, Chairman of Standish Group (Johnson, 2002). He showed a breakdown of features that are actually used in a typical delivered system:

- Features always used – 7%
- Features often used – 13%
- Features sometimes used – 16%
- Features rarely used – 19%
- Features never used – 45%

Therefore, all Agile frameworks have the concept of a clear definition of what stories are. All Agile frameworks have the concept of the customer collaborating with the team (see Section 11.1) to ensure alignment and focus. And all Agile frameworks have the concept of producing technically fit-for-purpose products.

13.2 FIT-FOR-PURPOSE DELIVERY

Teams need to ensure that any product is delivered in a fit-for-purpose way. This concept is well expressed in the following Lean software development principles (see Section 14.6):

Eliminate waste The three biggest wastes in software development are extra stories, stories constantly changing and the buffers created by crossing organisation boundaries.

Build in quality If defects are routinely found in the verification process, the development process is defective.

Create knowledge Planning is useful. Learning essential.

Defer commitment Abolish the idea that development should start with a complete specification.

Deliver fast Queues cause products to be passed between steps within the process. Typically there will be rigorous sign-off points to 'protect' the team next in the process against the risk of being blamed if something goes wrong with delivery. Communication will largely be via documentation across each of the teams in the delivery value chain, with the inherent communication difficulties that can cause.

Respect people Engaged, thinking people provide the most sustainable competitive advantage.

Optimise the whole Brilliant products emerge from a unique combination of opportunity and technology when viewed across the whole value chain

Sometimes the way an organisation is structured mirrors the delivery framework being used. Within a Waterfall-shaped organisation the risk is that teams form 'silos' within the key stages of the Waterfall delivery approach – which means that delivering anything across the value chain can become very complicated and full of 'waste' (see Section 6.2).

The risk is that where teams work in completely separated skill areas – e.g. analysts, designers, coders, testers – team members communicate by passing large documents across the 'silos', rather than communicating face-to-face (see Figure 13.1). In a team working with a silo mentality, these unseen boundaries can easily become barriers to effective communication and delivery.

Figure 13.1 Complex silo delivery

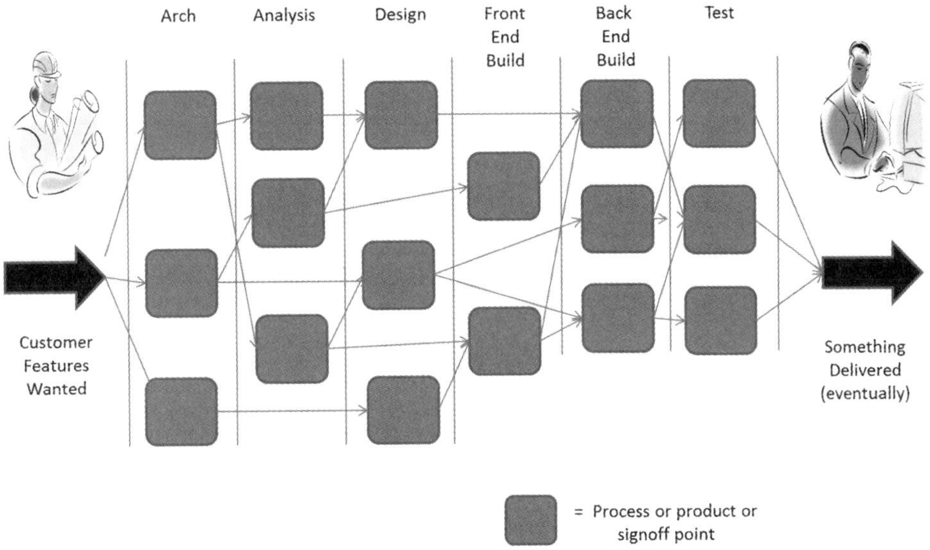

This causes the following risks to occur relating to the seven principles:

- **Eliminate waste:**
  - Extra stories – If the customer's experience across the complex silo delivery cycle has been that they don't get everything they want, they are likely to add in 'extra' stories up front with the intent that next time they will get what they want.
  - Stories constantly changing – If the complex silo delivery takes a lot of time it's likely that the customer's requirements will change.
  - Buffers – These are created by crossing organisation boundaries and requiring wait time to get sign-offs associated with crossing the organisational boundary.
- **Build in quality:** The end-to-end quality of the integrated product may not be tested until the end of the lifecycle with the inherent risk that significant functional or technical problems are found at that stage, at which it is too late to do anything about them.
- **Create knowledge:** Learning will typically occur within a siloed delivery organisation; however, it is more difficult to implement end-to-end learning.

- **Defer commitment:** Each silo will typically create detailed documentation that they can pass from one silo to the next. This drives the organisation to make all decisions as early as possible and not align to the concept of last responsible moment (see Section 9.2).

- **Deliver fast:** Queues cause products to be passed between steps within the process, and typically there will be rigorous sign-off points to 'protect' the team next in the process against the risk of being blamed if something goes wrong with delivery. Communication will largely be via documentation across each of the silos within the delivery value chain, with the inherent communication difficulties that causes.

- **Respect people:** The organisation can start to think of the value chain as a product line and the people within the production line as machines; this misses the huge competitive advantage that is provided by engaged people.

- **Optimise the whole:** Silo teams will concentrate on their own silos rather than across the value chain (from concept to cash), which means the required customer focus across the value chain is at risk.

13.2.1 Vertical slices

Vertical slicing is a core concept in all Agile frameworks (see Figure 13.2). Within a traditional delivery approach there will be delivery steps to achieve an outcome (e.g. analysis, design and so on within a Waterfall approach), and this drives horizontal slicing. In an Agile delivery the focus is on producing value-added product for the customer as

Figure 13.2 Vertical slicing

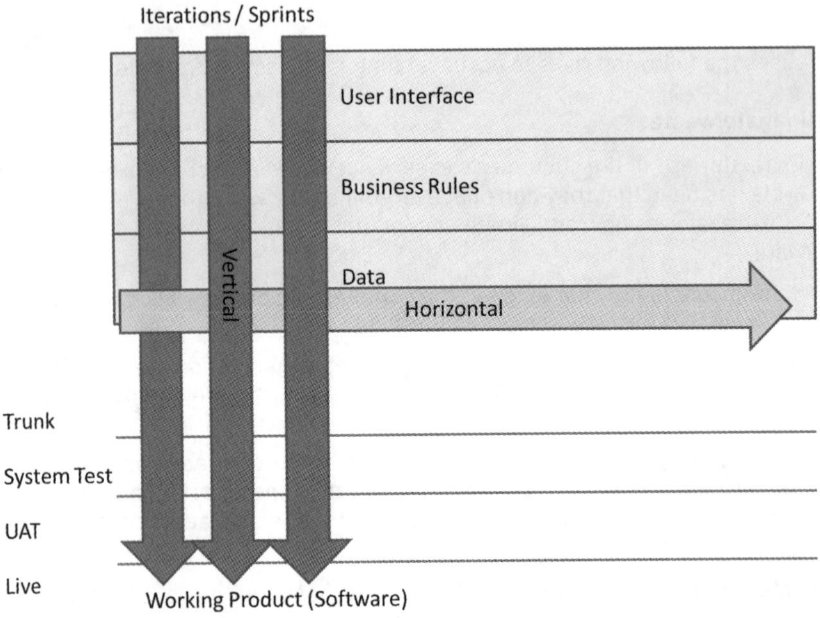

continuously as possible, which means teams focus on producing the highest value stories in vertical slices down the architecture.

Agile teams and customers collaborate to produce a single ordered list of what is required for delivery, expressed as stories. This gives a clear and visible indication of the preferred order of delivery and also a clear indication (via the story structure and acceptance criteria) of what makes that feature fit for purpose.

Teams are then structured as feature or component teams (see Section 6.2) so that they have the capability to deliver vertical slices across the value chain. In this case, the impact on the seven principles from Lean software development is as follows:

- **Eliminate waste:**
  - Extra stories – The customer and team continually collaborate to create the appropriate stories, which are delivered within short increments. The customer doesn't need to create extra stories because they are getting continuous delivery.
  - Stories constantly changing – Stories are delivered continuously within short timescales, which means it is unlikely that a story that is in production will change during the short timescale.
  - Buffers – The team works together, not requiring sign-offs between themselves.
- **Build in quality:** All types of testing are fully integrated throughout in all Agile frameworks.
- **Create knowledge:** The team works and continuously learns as a team focused on continuous delivery to the customer.
- **Defer commitment:** Agile aligns to the concept of last responsible moment (see Section 9.2).
- **Deliver fast:** Agile teams are focused on delivery of product increments within short timescales (typically a couple of weeks).
- **Respect people:** Ensuring that this behaviour is part of the organisation culture is one of the responsibilities of the Agile lead (see Section 6.3).
- **Optimise the whole:** Agile teams focus as a team on delivery across the whole value chain delivering value-add product to the customer in short time frames.

Simplicity is about focusing on value and removing all the impediments and disorder that distract from that objective.

PART 4
AGILE FRAMEWORKS

14 MAJOR AGILE FRAMEWORKS

This chapter does not pretend to describe all Agile frameworks in the market; rather this is a list of frameworks that are most popular in the market at the publication date. There are many other frameworks, many of which are named in the 'History of Agile' section (Section 1.1).

We define 'popular Agile frameworks' as the frameworks we have seen most widely used in the organisations we have interacted with over the last five years. All of the generic Agile practices that we have described in parts one to three of this book will be apparent within these frameworks.

14.1 EXTREME PROGRAMMING (XP)

14.1.1 The ethos of eXtreme Programming.

eXtreme Programming (XP; Beck, 2004) was conceived during the late 1990s to tackle the then-current methodologies' inability to deal with change. XP quickly became the dominant Agile methodology until Scrum overtook it in the early 2000s.

XP practices are based on a set of values and guiding principles; by understanding first the values, then the principles, teams can see why the XP practices are used. Without understanding the why, the practices lose their meaning and can easily slip.

XP takes proven practices and applies them in their purest, or most extreme form. It is a methodology for 'people coming together to develop software' and not specifically for programming (Beck, 2004).

There are many similarities between XP's values, principles and practices and the values of the Agile Manifesto. The now common Agile practices of stories, test-driven-development and continuous integration all originate from XP.

14.1.2 Values

Five values underpin the methods and behaviours applied in the principles and practices of XP.

14.1.2.1 Communication

Ambiguous or misinterpreted requirements, large unread documents, lack of face-to-face dialogue, isolated teams and other breakdowns in communication can lead directly to project delays or failure.

Communication is ingrained into XP – many of its practices cannot be done without communicating. Tasks such as planning and estimating must be performed together and are based on a verbal dialogue as opposed to a one-way document-based method. As a result of this approach, XP projects generally create less documentation than a Waterfall project.

XP teams are encouraged to communicate through practices such as co-location and pair-programming (see Section 14.1.4.7). Unit tests describe the behaviour of individual units of the overall system, thus becoming a method of communication themselves.

14.1.2.2 Feedback

A process that embraces change must receive feedback whenever possible.

Feedback within XP happens at many levels. Working in short iterations, teams have the opportunity for regular customer feedback. The state of functional tests shows the current development state of the project, while unit tests feed back information about the state of the code-base against people's expectations.

By interpreting feedback and applying learning to the system, XP is able to adapt quickly to changes at all levels.

14.1.2.3 Simplicity

This value is neatly summed up by the phrase 'do the simplest thing that could possibly work'. This translates to focusing on solutions for the current iteration of work and contributes to the rapid development of stories.

Simplicity is difficult to apply, and the best intentions may still result in unfortunate consequences or an inability to deliver. For example, developers may be tempted to add features into the code they believe will be required in the future. XP teams focus only on what is needed right now. Extra functionality or features can lead to extra work to be completed, such as functional tests, unit tests or unforeseen consequences in other areas of the system.

14.1.2.4 Respect

Respect must underpin the other values for them to be effective. This is directly related to the Agile Manifesto statement 'Individuals and interactions over processes and tools' as without respect within the team there will not be focused and effective delivery.

By respecting oneself as well as the other team members, people are more likely to feel confident that they are making a valuable contribution to the team and project as a whole.

14.1.2.5 Courage

It can take courage to stick to the values of XP. For example, it takes courage to highlight issues that could have an impact on the project, such as an architectural flaw late in the day. It takes courage to throw away code when you recognise that there is a better design. It takes courage to refactor another developer's code. It takes courage to fail and it takes courage to change.

Without the other values, courage can become recklessness. Only by being respectful, focusing on current development and communicating openly are actions courageous.

14.1.3 XP principles

XP's principles translate the abstract values into concrete practices and should be used to guide a project during development and when selecting appropriate, alternative or even new practices.

14.1.3.1 Fundamental principles

Rapid feedback
Seek feedback at the earliest possible moment, interpret it appropriately and apply learning from it back into the system. In practice this is achieved by the different testing activities, direct communication with the customer and the sharing of knowledge across the whole team.

Assume simplicity
Choose the simplest solution that could solve the problem. By applying the principle of simplicity to development, design and code becomes leaner, resulting in quicker development. It is only at the point when a particular feature is actually needed, that its design and code will be tackled. The phrase 'You Ain't Gonna Need It' (YAGNI) was coined to embody this principle.

Applied blindly or in isolation, this principle can lead to a messy, hard-to-work-with system. Therefore it needs to be used alongside other practices such as refactoring, unit tests and continuous integration (see Section 8.10).

Incremental change
By working incrementally, teams focus on manageably sized tasks. Two-week iterations and their goals are much easier to focus on than a six month project.

By receiving regular and frequent feedback, many small, deliberate changes can be made. Large projects are broken up into small releases, difficult problems are broken up into a collection of smaller simpler problems and writing small tests creates code. It is even recommended that the introduction of XP practices themselves is applied in small manageable steps.

Embracing change
In software development change is a reality. Large, up-front plans and designs are costly to change. While this principle does not mean that all changes must be accepted, it encourages people to find new ways of working with change. So, for example, there will be no large up-front designs – instead teams will design as the project develops. Also, there will be no large requirements documents – teams will plan only as far as the next release. Essentially, this principle says that change is to be expected and that teams need to have a process that works with it.

Quality work
An XP team is committed to the principle of doing a good job. This can mean technically, or this can mean by keeping the core values and principles at the heart of what it does.

By producing quality work, members of an XP team will be proud of their contribution to the project, which becomes a motivating factor.

Sacrificing quality will only have a negative effect on a project. As one of the fundamental principles of XP, it should not be optional.

14.1.3.2 Further principles

These principles are more specific to particular situations.

- Teach learning: XP teams use their experience to apply XP practices (see below) to the appropriate degree. If some practices are less known, strategies are devised so team members can learn.

- Small initial investment: With a tight budget on a project, there is more likely to be a strong focus from both a requirements and technology perspective. Often this sort of environment can generate innovation.

- Play to win: The actions of individuals on an XP team are intended to help the team and project succeed or 'win', rather than to protect the individual from blame in the event of failure.

- Concrete experiments: Decisions should be underpinned by the result of experiments to reduce risk.

- Open and honest communication: Team members should be encouraged to communicate in an open and honest manner, even if it means delivering bad or uncomfortable news. Often, if team members do not feel able to do this, it is a sign of a larger cultural problem.

- Work with people's instincts, not against them: The XP team trust their instincts to do the right thing.

- Accepted responsibility: Individuals are not told what to do, they take responsibility when required. This is part of self-organisation.

- Local adaptation: XP should be adapted to the respective environment. It may not be possible to follow all the practices exactly.

- Travel light: Unnecessary tools and practices should be avoided. Tools are tempting but they can also restrict project practices.

- Honest measurement: Metrics that are of no value to the team or project should be avoided, and metrics that are used should be made visible.

14.1.4 Practices

14.1.4.1 The planning game

The main planning activity in XP takes place at both release and iteration level.

In release planning, the customer will translate requirements into **user-stories** and the team will estimate how long each will take (**exploration phase**). Based on the business value, combined with the estimates, the customer will decide the scope and date of the next release (**commitment phase**).

While the exploration and commitment phases may be completed in a single whole-team meeting, the final phase of release planning, called the **steering phase**, is played over the remaining time to the release. In this phase, the project is guided, or **steered**, based on feedback from both the customer and development. During the steering phase the team works in short iterations. Based on the user-story estimates and their business value, the customer selects enough stories to fill the iteration. The team then identifies the individual tasks required to deliver each story.

The team aims to deliver working software at the end of the iteration. Feedback from each iteration's delivery is used to **steer** the project. Both the customer and team have opportunities during the steering phase to make changes. The customer can add new user-stories, which receive a development estimate. In doing this, the customer must indicate which existing stories will be replaced.

The team can adjust their estimates. If the re-estimation is isolated in one story, then only the current iteration may be affected; however if the re-estimation has to be applied to the remaining user-stories, the release plan itself may be affected. In this case the scope or date of the release will need to be reassessed.

14.1.4.2 Small releases

XP teams should aim to create releases of valuable functionality as quickly as possible. It is the customer's responsibility to identify the functional release increments, moving away from the idea that the system cannot be released until complete.

By identifying small increments of functionality, releases can start to gather feedback that can be used in steering the system's subsequent development, as well as potentially delivering business value early.

14.1.4.3 Metaphor

By creating a metaphor, the whole team can form an understanding of the system, its elements and their relationships. To keep a metaphor relevant, its language should be used throughout the project. This allows the team to relate back to the metaphor, which is useful when describing technical changes. The metaphor may be used in place of, or as part of, the system architecture.

For example, many e-commerce applications have used the shopping cart as a metaphor to discuss requirements; another common e-commerce metaphor is to consider the product to be built using an auction metaphor (e.g. eBay).

14.1.4.4 Simple design

The design applied by the developers must be as simple as possible, satisfying only the requirements for the functionality being implemented.

The design must still satisfy any relevant quality criteria or standards, and it may require a number of refactoring exercises (see Section 8.10.1) before the simplest design reveals itself, but it means the code will be easier to understand, test and modify.

14.1.4.5 Testing

All **stories** are to have automated tests (see Section 8.10).

Automated functional tests, with criteria specified as part of each user-story, provide the customer with two key benefits:

1. Indications of progress as new tests are shown to be successful.
2. Confidence in the system as existing tests are shown to be successful.

The team will be driven by tests. Test Driven Development is the practice of writing a unit test before creating the code itself.

14.1.4.6 Refactoring

Refactoring is the process of simplifying the internal structure of code without affecting its external behaviour (see Section 8.10.1).

When used in combination with test-driven development, developers iterate code once a test is written to arrive at the simplest possible solution. The unit-test verifies that the code still operates as expected.

14.1.4.7 Pair programming

Code is created by **two** developers using **one** machine. While the developer at the keyboard is focused on creating the current test and code, the other is thinking from a different perspective – for example, they may be considering how the code fits into the overall solution or thinking of different test scenarios. After a period of time or at a convenient point, the developers swap places.

Pair programming has a number of benefits:

- Conversation during the process helps to quickly move the solution on.
- Knowledge is shared as developers pair with different individuals.
- Code is reviewed in real-time; teams that practise pair programming often eschew code reviews.
- The practice promotes collective code ownership.

14.1.4.8 Collective ownership

Developers can improve any part of the code at any time.

When performed in concert with pair programming and good testing, knowledge of the system is shared very quickly. This practice also avoids code becoming owned by individuals, which can lead to bottlenecks in development and poorly designed code.

14.1.4.9 Continuous integration

The codebase should be integrated and automated tests run frequently.

Developers working locally on their machines should check-in their changes frequently, ensuring that code conflicts are identified and resolved quickly.

In tandem with this, the codebase should be integrated automatically each time a change is checked in. On a successful build of the system, automated tests should be executed. The results of both the build and the test run should be clearly visible, with any failures acted on immediately.

14.1.4.10 Forty-hour week

To ensure that team members remain creative, enthusiastic and perform at their best, XP teams must aim to work at a sustainable pace. XP does not forbid overtime, but it has a clear rule – *You can't work a second week of overtime.* The need for overtime should be mitigated by the other practices of XP; in particular the feedback aspects should allow problems to be discovered and addressed early rather than uncovered late in the day. The constant need for overtime on an XP project is an indication that estimates may need re-examining (see Section 14.1.4.1*)*.

14.1.4.11 On-site customer

A real customer should sit with the team. This person will be someone who will use the system, who has the knowledge and authority to answer questions and who can provide business related clarification so that issues don't block the progress of the iteration. It is expected that the customer will still carry out their normal day-to-day role, just co-located with the team.

14.1.4.12 Coding standards

A common coding standard, agreed by all developers, must be adopted across the team. The standard should refer to the other practices, such as simple design, and where possible identify established coding principles such as the SOLID principles (Martin, 2000). As the project progresses, the code will become identified by team coding style as opposed to any individual's coding style. This benefits the whole team, removing one of the barriers to **collective ownership**.

14.2 SCRUM

According to the State of Agile Development Survey (VersionOne, n.d.), Scrum or various Scrum variants are the most popular Agile frameworks, achieving 72 per cent. This section provides a more detailed approach of the most significant practices.

14.2.1 Overview

The Scrum framework (Schwaber and Sutherland, n.d.), or simply Scrum, is an iterative and incremental Agile framework, which is based on the three pillars of empirical process control, Transparency, Inspection and Adaptation (see Section 2.6.1):

- Transparency: provide visibility to all stakeholders, customers and anyone else responsible for the outcome.

- Inspection: check in a timely fashion on how well a product is progressing towards its goals.

- Adaptation: adjust the process to minimise deviation from those goals.

The Scrum framework consists of a set of values, roles, activities and artefacts that form a holistic approach to delivering products. The people-centric framework adjusts to the characteristics of each environment, making every implementation unique within IT and non-IT-related environments. The first public announcement of Scrum (presented as **methodology**) took place in the Object-Oriented Programming, Systems, Languages and Applications (OOPSLA) conference in 1995, by its originators Jeff Sutherland and Ken Schwaber (Sutherland and Schwaber, 2013).

14.2.2 Scrum roles

A Scrum team has three roles with specific properties and responsibilities:

- ScrumMaster.
- Product owner.
- Development team.

The ScrumMaster facilitates the adoption of Scrum through continuous coaching and guidance, leading the Scrum team to high-performance and using the framework to inspect and adapt. The product owner defines what will be delivered in what order (via the product backlog), and the development team defines how to deliver what has been asked for and how long it will take (via the sprint backlog). The development team is a self-organising, cross-functional and collaborative entity, which aims to deliver the goals agreed with the product owner.

14.2.2.1 ScrumMaster

The ultimate ownership of Scrum values, principles and practices lies with the ScrumMaster. The servant-leadership approach (see Section 6.3) differentiates this role from traditional project management and development management roles, exercising no control and authority over the team (Adkins, 2010).

The ScrumMaster acts in a mentoring and coaching capacity similar to a change agent, providing process leadership and facilitating the use of Scrum at the team level to enable (amongst others) self-organisation and high-performance skills. In addition, the ScrumMaster also works at the organisation level, mitigating impediments towards the adoption of an organisation-specific Scrum approach.

Through specific activities and continuous coaching, the ScrumMaster helps the development team overcome impediments, resolve issues of internal or external nature and make best use of the lightweight and flexible framework. Blocking issues beyond the remit of the development team are addressed and escalated by the ScrumMaster, allowing the team to concentrate on the sprint goal. External interference/noise should be eliminated, as the ScrumMaster acts as a team armour in line with Agile Manifesto principle number five: *Build projects around motivated individuals. Give them the environment and support they need, and trust them to get the job done.*

A ScrumMaster is like a sheepdog, guiding and shepherding the team.

By adopting a continuous improvement mentality, the ScrumMaster challenges norms of development that inhibit performance, while maintaining constant focus on the goal of the current objectives in line with Agile Manifesto principle number 12: *At regular intervals, the team reflects on how to become more effective, then tunes and adjusts accordingly.*

In summary, the ScrumMaster is responsible for the following:

- The success of the Scrum process.
- Establishing Scrum practices and rules, shielding the team and removing obstacles.
- Ensuring that the Scrum team is fully functional and productive.
- Enabling close cooperation across all roles and functions.
- Ensuring that the Scrum process is followed, including effective daily Scrum meetings, sprint reviews, retrospectives and planning meetings.
- Leading and coaching the organisation in adopting Scrum.
- Assisting the product owner and finding effective product backlog management techniques.

14.2.2.2 Product owner

The product owner is the 'empowered central point of product leadership' within a Scrum team (Rubin, 2013). The main responsibilities of the role are defining and prioritising Product Backlog Items (PBIs) as well as maximising the value of the product overall.

Communication boundaries should not exist in a Scrum team, and such decisions are not made in isolation: requirement elaboration and prioritisation is supported by frequent contributions from the development team. Being the main liaison between the development team and the rest of the organisation, product owners are the 'single voice of the customer', collaborating with product managers, business analysts, customers and other stakeholders to determine requirements (Schwaber, 2004). It falls within their remit to maintain and effectively communicate a clear vision and set of objectives for the sprint and the release to all participants.

In addition, product owners have outward-looking activities (e.g. stakeholder management), including participating in strategic meetings, portfolio management sessions and cross-departmental discovery exercises. Despite their busy schedule, product owners must be readily available to answer questions on a just-in-time basis and steer the development team to the right direction through face-to-face communication.

Here is a summary of activities for the product owner:

- Identifying relative value on the PBIs.
- Communicating the vision of the business to the team and the vision of the team to the business.

- Defining available budget.

- Setting goals for the sprints and releases.

- Participating in the sprint planning and release planning meetings.

- Elaborating PBIs on a just-in-time basis with the team.

- Accepting PBIs.

- Accepting the sprint/release.

- Deciding when to release.

- Defining the features of the product via PBIs (mainly stories (see Section 7.1))

- Setting development schedule by ordering the product backlog.

- Adjusting PBIs and prioritising every sprint as needed.

- Ensuring return on investment.

- Gaining insight and assurance the product is meeting its goals through deep and broad feedback.

14.2.2.3 Development team

The nature of the development team in Scrum is fundamentally different from teams in traditional, Waterfall and command-and-control settings. In such models, existing organisational structures promote functional silos, communication barriers and wasteful handovers.

The diverse and cross-functional collection of specialisations relies on a matrix organisational structure that potentially comprises coders, testers, architects, product managers, business analysts, user experience designers, other specialist and supporting personnel, and so forth – basically everyone required to get the PBI to 'done' status.

Self-organisation, a critical aspect in Scrum, is an evolving characteristic of the development team. The team is allowed to determine the best manner to realise the requirements that the product owner defined and prioritised in the form of sprint goal in line with Agile Manifesto principle number 11: *The best architectures, requirements, and designs emerge from self-organising teams*. According to the *Scrum guide* (Sutherland and Schwaber, 2013), the ideal team size should be small enough to maintain sufficient collaboration and communication levels, and large enough to complete significant, high-quality, working software items within given sprints (Agile Manifesto principle number 7: *Working software is the primary measure of progress*). The typical number of members in a development team spans from 5 to 9 members (rule of thumb: 7 ± 2 developers). Smaller teams are likely to experience skill constraints, inhibiting the delivery of potentially releasable increments. On the other hand, larger groups are unable to manage the complexity introduced for empirical methods.

The responsibilities of the development team are summarised below:

- Working with the product owner, ensuring that PBIs are understood and realised appropriately.

- Defining emergent architectures while maintaining quality at the agreed level.

- Self-organising, cross-functional with no predetermined roles.
- Seven plus or minus two people – all skills required to get PBIs to 'done'.
- Lots of face-to-face communication.
- Responsible for organising tasks and committing to work.
- Authority to do whatever is needed to meet commitment.
- Demonstrates work results to the product owner and stakeholders.
- Has the right to do everything within the boundaries of the delivery standards and guidelines to reach the sprint/release goal.

14.2.3 Scrum activities and artefacts

14.2.3.1 Scrum framework

This most popular and lightweight Agile framework follows a particular process (see Figure 14.1), which is outlined in the following paragraphs.

Figure 14.1 Scrum process

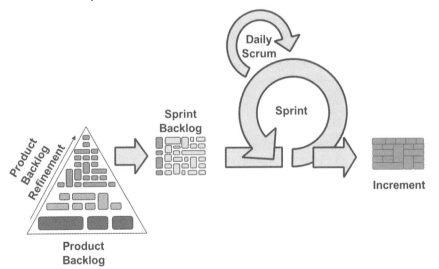

Traditionally, the strategic intent of the delivery is communicated through the product owner to the Scrum team. Product backlog items may include critical contextual information and supplementary documentation. As the development effort required to realise all PBIs in the product vision can be large, the Scrum team engages in a decomposition and prioritisation activity, called refinement or grooming, which breaks down items into a number of smaller, clearer and more concise items that are deemed 'ready' (see Section 10.2) for sprint planning, which the development team can turn into product increments, ideally within two to five days. The team will refine the PBIs guided by prioritisation. The product backlog must be prioritised, ordered and estimated, as it is used for planning and forecasting future sprints or releases. Items further down the product backlog will be less well understood and therefore estimates will be less precise.

Development time is divided into time-boxes with the duration of no more than one month, with a preference for a shorter timescale known as **sprints**. Each sprint starts with a planning exercise, named **sprint planning**, which determines the set of prioritised PBIs that the development team is likely to realise in a collaborative manner. The team plan how they will develop the product increment from the PBIs, and create a sprint backlog, which contains the known tasks required to create an increment for each PBI planned for the coming sprint. Nevertheless, changes should be expected as the team goes through the 'cone of uncertainty' (see Section 2.5) and more information surfaces.

It is imperative that the team feels comfortable with the items listed in the sprint backlog and commits to its execution to the best of their abilities. Commitment is an essential element of Scrum, as the development team commits to the sprint goal which is typically a subset of the PBIs in the sprint, the sprint backlog is always a forecast, the sprint goal is a commitment. Throughout the duration of the sprint, the development team focuses on PBI design, implementation, integration, testing and documentation (sprint execution), which concludes with two inspect-and-adapt events: the sprint review and sprint retrospective.

In the sprint review, which is the public end to the sprint, the Scrum team demonstrates the implemented PBIs to the business participants and gathers direct feedback. During the sprint retrospective, the 'private end to the sprint', the team pursues a process improvement exercise, identifying areas for improvement. The outcome from the session should be an actionable list of improvements, which should be part of the subsequent sprint backlog.

14.2.3.2 Product backlog

The fundamental focus of Scrum on early and continuous delivery of valuable software depends partly on a Lean and transparent requirements model known as the product backlog, which supports the demands of external stakeholders and team members (see Agile Manifesto principle number 1: *Our highest priority is to satisfy the customer through early and continuous delivery of valuable software*). The product owner, with assistance from the ScrumMaster, Scrum team and business stakeholders, is ultimately responsible for defining, elaborating, sequencing and communicating added-value work in an ordered fashion. Work items are sorted in descending order, with relatively higher value items appearing at the top and lower value items appearing towards the bottom. The process of eliciting and ranking requirements is called value-based decomposition and prioritisation.

Product backlog items may be defined at differing levels of clarity and understanding as they are refined prior to sprint planning, incorporating changes based on feedback and time-boxed investigative work ('spikes' – see Section 7.1.3).

As mentioned before, requirements definition and progressive elaboration does not occur in isolation. The product owner liaises with internal and external stakeholders to define the PBIs. Regardless of the prioritisation scheme used, all stakeholders should comprehend the factors associated with the current sequence, such as relative business value, risk involved, available knowledge, return of investment, expected monetary value, and so on. The evolution of the product backlog, known as backlog refinement (also backlog grooming), is an activity that takes place very frequently within Scrum teams. PBIs are refined (broken down), added, removed, modified and re-prioritised according to the constantly changing business needs and competitive landscape. Throughout the course of development, the product owner and the development team gather useful information via feedback loops (see 'sprint review' below), which has impact on the PBIs and their priority.

14.2.3.3 Sprints

Product development work (or any type of work in non-IT environments) in Scrum is performed in time-boxed (time-limited) iterations or cycles, producing a potentially releasable increment that contributes to the value stream.

The suggested time-box should be a maximum of a month with a preference for a shorter timescale. Most development teams start at two weeks and then change from that length if required. Although the duration of all sprints should remain constant, it could be revisited periodically, as a part of continuous improvement discussions between the ScrumMaster and the development team. Each sprint is followed by another sprint, forming a cadence, which is considered the 'Agile' heartbeat used to coordinate various Scrum-related events and activities, such as sprint planning meetings, sprint reviews, retrospectives, and other non-Scrum-related tasks.

Each sprint has a sprint goal, meaning a set of objectives mutually agreed between the development team and the product owner. Fundamentally, altering the goal mid-sprint is not an acceptable practice, as changes in sprint scope disorientate the Scrum team.

14.2.3.4 Sprint planning

Prior to any development, each sprint starts with a session when team plan their work. During this significant planning activity, known as the sprint planning meeting, the Scrum team accumulates knowledge in a collaborative manner and the product owner defines most added-value PBIs from the product backlog. As the Scrum team agrees, the selected work items are scheduled for execution.

Information sharing, conversations and other collaborative activities should be specific to planning. Therefore, it is common practice that sprint planning follows a predetermined agenda.

Within 'sprint planning part 1' the product owner initially defines the set of achievements, named the 'sprint goal', which should be accomplished at the end of the sprint, in agreement with the team. This high-level goal acts as a driver of the conversations and decisions that will follow. The development team commit to the sprint goal, the product owner commits to not add PBIs or any other noise to the development team during the sprint so they can focus on delivering the sprint goal.

Many development teams proceed into further decomposition of the chosen product backlog items into technical tasks, this is known as 'sprint planning part 2'. Through conversations, team members have better visibility and understanding of the effort needed to realise the PBI at hand. This approach achieves just-in-time planning that eliminates wasteful up-front discussions. Development teams do sufficient design and planning to be confident of completing the work in the sprint. Work to be done in the early days is broken down into units of one day or less.

The collection of PBIs chosen, including their technical tasks and estimations, make up the **sprint backlog**, which will change throughout the course of the sprint as the team update their estimates. The team own the sprint backlog and must maintain it throughout the sprint, guiding the development team in their pursuit of the sprint goal.

14.2.3.5 Sprinting

Following the commitment of the development team to the mutually agreed sprint goal, sprint execution starts. The main focus of the development team during delivery, facilitated and coached by the ScrumMaster, is to implement the product backlog items through tasks.

The development team is empowered to define task-level work without interference and follows the necessary steps to get the PBIs 'done' (see Section 10.2.1).

14.2.3.6 Daily Scrum

Face-to-face communication and synchronisation meetings are essentials in Agile. Similarly in Scrum, the development team participates in a recurring meeting, which takes place on a daily basis at an agreed time. Known as the daily Scrum, it is a strictly time-boxed session, up to 15 minutes, which allows the team members to understand current progress, synchronise activities and share information about obstacles hindering progress towards the sprint goal. Daily Scrums have strong roots in 'Kaizen' culture (continuous improvement – Lean) and are frequently referred to as daily stand-ups, as team members usually remain standing throughout its duration, in order to keep conversations concise and the time short.

The standard agenda of a daily Scrum, which is facilitated by the ScrumMaster, consists of three straightforward questions, which are answered by each participant:

- What did I do yesterday?
- What do I plan to do today?
- What is getting in my way?

The 'what did I do yesterday?' question gives the opportunity to every participant to outline what they have accomplished since the last daily Scrum. This is followed by the 'what do I plan to do today?' question, which provides visibility of what the next steps are to the rest of the team and encourages a commitment between peers. The combination of the first two questions highlights a sequence of events that are important for all team members to synchronise. Finally, the 'what is getting in my way?' question allows members to raise concerns about current progress, brings impediments to the attention of the team and allows for modifications to anything that is impeding progress should these be considered necessary. The ScrumMaster plays a pivotal role in removing any obstacles to moving forward.

According to Jean Tabaka (2006), the questions above could be posed differently, emphasising the commitment amongst team members:

- What did I commit to do for all of us yesterday?
- What am I going to commit to do for the team today?
- What may be preventing me from meeting my commitment to the team till the next daily scrum?

To further focus on the benefits of the actionable status information, Craig Larman (2003) suggested two additional questions for daily Scrums:

- Have any additional tasks been identified for this sprint (in the sprint backlog)?
- Have you learnt or decided anything new which would be of relevance to some of the team members?

Daily Scrums improve communication and provide an excellent platform for adaptive daily planning and self-organisation. As they significantly contribute to the progression of development effort, participation is anticipated. Nevertheless, to keep the meetings efficient, yet ensure that communication flows effectively, the rules of the daily Scrum distinguish which members should actively participate from those that solely observe. Daily Scrums are open to stakeholders outside the strict boundaries of the Scrum team; however, they observe as listeners rather than contributors. The Scrum team, including the product owner (if the team have agreed the product owner will be present), must participate as they are all committed to the sprint goal.

14.2.3.7 Definition of done

See Section 10.2.1.

14.2.3.8 Sprint review

In the course of each sprint, the development team adopts an inward-looking approach towards development, focusing on achieving the sprint goal through commitment and self-organisation. At the finish line, each sprint concludes with two additional inspect-and-adapt activities: the sprint review and the sprint retrospective. Particularly in sprint review, the team has an excellent platform to engage in inspect-and-adapt conversations amongst its members and with the rest of the organisation.

The inspect-and-adapt activity consists of presentations/reviews of the completed sprint backlog items within the context of the product vision and future development scope. The current status of development effort becomes apparent to all participants, allowing everyone to steer the scope of future sprints to the right business direction. The bidirectional nature of information flow improves visibility between the Scrum team and business stakeholders (Rubin, 2013). The former has better clarity and appreciation of the business requirements through direct feedback, whereas the latter understand the work 'done' in the potentially shippable increment. Sprint reviews are also an opportunity for the Scrum team to showcase their technical achievements, which frequently has a positive effect on team morale and empowerment.

14.2.3.9 Sprint retrospective

In Agile environments, where continuous improvement and Kaizen culture thrive, sprint retrospectives are the activities which celebrate process optimisation, team building and collaboration building activities. The last ceremony in Scrum – before the end of the sprint – is essential in identifying opportunities for performance and collaboration improvements, deciding on adjustments of the current delivery approach and understanding any knowledge and skill-set gaps. It also strengthens the bond amongst the Scrum team members, who 'continue their path from divergence to convergence' (Tabaka, 2006).

As the Scrum team reflects and identifies opportunities for improvement, the ScrumMaster facilitates the process of engaging the Scrum team to commit to such process improvement actions. All action points should be undertaken during the following sprint.

14.3 DSDM

DSDM is an Agile project management and delivery framework from the DSDM Consortium (DSDM Consortium, 2014b), of which the Agile project framework is the latest version. In the DSDM Consortium's own words:

> We're all about scalable Agile delivery of projects and programmes with the right amount of governance and control that enables successful innovation.

> (DSDM Consortium, 2014b)

Many other Agile frameworks describe an approach that works well for delivery of a product, but they do not provide the governance that is required when working within a project governance structure. DSDM provides the governance necessary to run an effective Agile project and deliver the product. DSDM is also equally applicable to IT and non-IT projects (by replacing the 'working software above comprehensive documentation' line on the Agile Manifesto with 'working **solution** above comprehensive documentation'.

DSDM defines a philosophy that is supported by eight principles, a development process, roles and responsibilities and a comprehensive set of products, all of which are supported by five practices.

14.3.1 The DSDM philosophy and eight principles

The DSDM philosophy is that:

> ... best business value emerges when projects are aligned to clear business goals, deliver frequently and involve the collaboration of motivated and empowered people.

> (DSDM Consortium, 2014b)

The philosophy is supported by the eight guiding principles; these provide the mind-set and behaviours needed for a project to be successful.

Principle 1 – Focus on the business need Deliver what the business wants when the business needs it.

Principle 2 – Deliver on time By working in time-boxes and applying MSCW the team will always make a delivery on time.

Principle 3 – Collaborate Teams who collaborate will outperform those who don't. Collaboration increases team understanding, improves speed to deliver and creates a sense of shared ownership.

Principle 4 – Never compromise on quality Aim to deliver the agreed level of quality from the beginning of the project through to the end.

Principle 5 – Build incrementally from firm foundations Building from firm foundations is critical to be able to deliver value early and continue to add value throughout a project. Firm foundations are created by doing the appropriate level of investigation up front – enough design up front (EDUF), rather than no design up front (NDUF) or big design up front (BDUF). This is particularly important for large or complex projects/programmes or in large or complex organisations.

Principle 6 – Develop iteratively Iterative development allows teams to converge on the best solution by using a cycle of Thought, Action and Conversation.

Principle 7 – Communicate continuously and clearly Poor communication is often the cause of project failure. DSDM uses many processes and practices to support effective communication.

Principle 8 – Demonstrate control Any project management methodology needs to be in control, as do all roles working on an Agile project. DSDM demonstrates control by involving the whole team in creation of plans which are visible to all, and then by measuring progress through focus on delivery of products, rather than completed activities.

14.3.2 The DSDM roles and responsibilities

DSDM provides a fuller set of roles than other Agile frameworks, to reflect the additional complexity of a project environment. The roles are split into three main groups, project level, solution development team level and supporting level (see Figure 14.2). A person can take more than one role, and a role can be covered by more than one person. It is therefore important to identify and communicate who will be taking responsibility for which roles.

The project level roles are:

- **Business sponsor** The business sponsor is the person who is funding the project.

- **Business visionary** The business visionary provides the team with the 'big picture' – the context and strategic direction to ensure the solution delivers benefit to the business. This role should be held by a single individual, since a project needs a single clear vision to avoid confusion and misdirection.

141

- **Project manager** The project manager coordinates all aspects of management of the project at a high level, but in line with the DSDM concept of empowerment, the project manager is expected to leave the detailed planning of the actual delivery of the product(s) to the members of the solution development team.

- **Technical coordinator** As the project's technical authority, the technical coordinator ensures that the solution/technical roles work in a consistent way, that the project is technically coherent and meets the desired technical quality standards.

Figure 14.2 DSDM roles

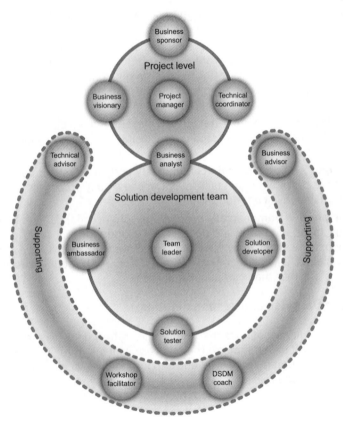

The solution development team roles are:

- **Business ambassador** The business ambassador is a key role. During iterative development, the business ambassador is the main day-to-day decision maker on behalf of the business. For this reason the business ambassador needs to be someone who is respected by their business peers and who has sufficient seniority, empowerment and credibility to make decisions on behalf of the business, in terms of ensuring the evolving solution is fit-for-business-purpose.

- **Business analyst** The business analyst is both active in supporting the project-level roles and fully integrated with the solution development team. The business analyst facilitates the relationship between the business and technical roles, ensuring accurate and appropriate decisions are made on the evolving solution on a day-to-day basis.

- **Team leader** The team leader is the servant-leader for the team, making sure the team follow their development process and removing impediments for the team. The team leader should foster a self-organising team.

- **Solution developer** The solution developer collaborates with the other solution development team roles to interpret business requirements and translate them into a solution that meets functional and non-functional needs.

- **Solution tester** The solution tester is fully integrated with the team and throughout the project performs testing in accordance with the agreed strategy for technical testing.

There are four supporting roles:

- **Technical advisor** The technical advisor supports the team by providing specific and often specialist technical input to the project from the perspective of those responsible for operational change management, operational support, ongoing maintenance of the solution etc.

- **Business advisor** The business advisor provides specific and, often, specialist input to solution development or solution testing – a business subject matter expert. The business advisor will normally be an intended user or beneficiary of the solution or may be a representative of a focus group.

- **Workshop facilitator** The workshop facilitator is responsible for managing the workshop process and is the catalyst for preparation and communication. The facilitator is responsible for the workshop process, organising and facilitating a session that allows the participants to achieve the workshop objective.

- **DSDM coach** Where a team has limited experience of using DSDM, the role of the DSDM coach is key to helping team members to get the most out of the approach, within the context and constraints of the wider organisation in which they work.

14.3.3 The DSDM process

The DSDM process has several phases (see Figure 14.3).

- **Pre-project** The pre-project phase is a very short one, where the idea for a project is formed. Depending on the project and organisation this may be a formal terms-of-reference document, or something as simple as an email.

- **Feasibility** The feasibility phase takes the information from the pre-project phase and starts to create outline requirements, potential solution(s) at a high level, an outline plan and an outline business case. Just enough needs to be done to establish if the project is feasible.

- **Foundations** The foundations phase takes the output from the feasibility phase and adds enough detail to the requirements, solution and plan for there to be a sufficiently firm foundation for the project to go into development.

Figure 14.3 DSDM process

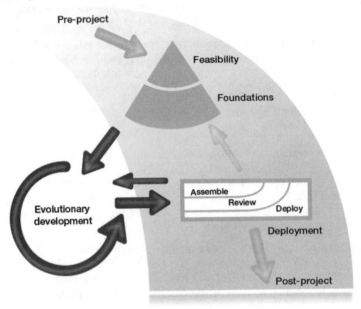

The pre-project, feasibility and foundations phases are sequential. The business case is reassessed at each point to ensure the project is still good to go ahead.

- **Evolutionary development** Building on the firm foundations that have been established for the project, the evolutionary development phase evolves the solution, working within time-boxes. The solution development team(s) apply practices such as iterative development, time-boxing, and MSCW prioritisation, together with modelling and facilitated workshops, to converge on an accurate solution that meets the business need and is also built in the right way from a technical viewpoint.

- **Deployment** The objective of the deployment phase is to release one or more increments of the solution into operational use. Each deployment may be the final solution or a subset of the final solution. The ongoing project viability should also be assessed. If this is the last deployment, the project will be formally closed.

- **Post-project** Post-project is the assessment of whether the solution has delivered the expected benefits. This means it may need to happen 3 to 6 months after deployment so that the benefits can start to emerge. The business sponsor and business visionary are responsible for validating that the business benefits have been received.

14.3.4 The products (a summary)

DSDM defines a complete set of products that can be used while managing an Agile project delivery. It is often not necessary to use all of the products defined by DSDM; instead it is better to tailor the products into the leanest possible subset.

The products can be categorised into three types:

- **Business products** – prioritised requirements, business vision, business case etc.
- **Management products** – plans, management foundations, control information e.g. risk log and review records etc.
- **Solution products** – the solution itself, supported by lean and timely documentation such as test records, an up-to-date definition of the solution architecture definition.

DSDM provides an explanation of when in the project delivery lifecycle each project should be created and updated, and additional detail on the purpose and constituent parts of each product.

14.3.5 The five practices

DSDM identifies five practices that help make a project delivery successful:

- **MSCW** – is a requirements prioritisation technique used in DSDM (see Section 7.1.4). MSCW stands for Must have, Should have, Could have, Won't have (this time). Ensuring the right balance of MSCW priorities helps build successful predictable projects.
- **Facilitated workshops** – use an interactive workshop environment, effective group dynamics and visual aids to extract high quality information in a compressed time frame in order to meet a predetermined set of deliverables. Workshops help build a collaborative working environment and group consensus, an essential part of Agile. It is good practice to have an independent facilitator who has no stake in the outcome of the workshop. The facilitator's role is to manage the workshop process, which then allows the participants to focus on providing high quality content, based on their personal knowledge and expertise in the subject being discussed. A well-organised facilitator will send out workshop information in advance, especially where participants need to do some pre-work or investigation before the workshop. After the workshop it is important to communicate any output to all attendees.
- **Modelling** – is another practice that helps build effective communication. 'A picture is worth a thousand words.' Creating a model, whether this is a simple drawing on a flip chart, a process flow, a scaled model, or even a prototype, allows people to see what is being discussed or proposed. Models allow people

145

to visualise a solution far better than reading a list of requirements, and this in turn allows people to create or challenge ideas.

- **Time-boxing** – most Agile methods would describe time-boxing as a simple fixed period of time to develop the product. DSDM, however, focuses more detail around time-boxing and recognises two different styles – a free-format style and a DSDM structured time-box. For both styles, DSDM recommends a fixed length of time, typically 2–4 weeks, and both styles are topped with a kick-off stage and tailed with a close-out stage (see Figure 14.4).

Figure 14.4 The DSDM structured (three iteration) time-box

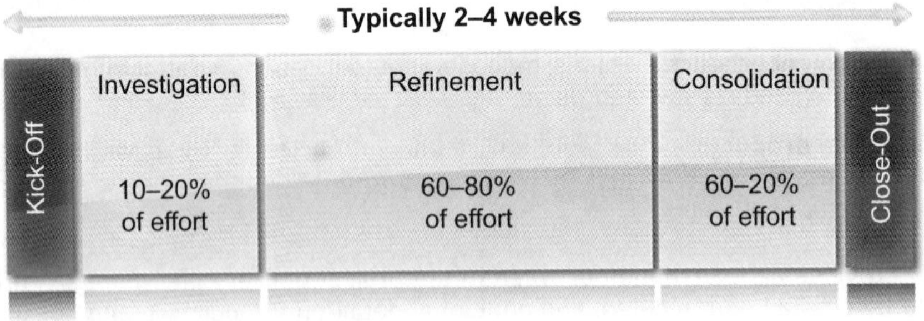

Typically 2–4 weeks

Kick-Off	Investigation	Refinement	Consolidation	Close-Out
	10–20% of effort	60–80% of effort	60–20% of effort	

A DSDM structured time-box can be helpful where the business availability is limited, as the structure is very useful to allow forward planning of the times when the business ambassador will attend specific planning, feedback and review sessions.

- **Kick-off** (1–3 hours) is a short session at the beginning of a time-box to understand the time-box objectives.

- **Investigation** (10–20 per cent of time-box) is where the team look at the requirements and define what work needs to be done to meet the objective.

- **Refinement** (60–80 per cent of time-box) is where the product is developed.

- **Consolidation** (10–20 per cent of time-box) is where the team double-check everything is complete and meets all acceptance criteria.

- **Close-out** (1–3 hours) is where the project visionary and technical coordinator formally accept the product.

Investigation, refinement and consolidation each complete with a review.

The free format time-box (Figure 14.5) also starts with a kick-off and finishes with a close-out. However, in between, there may be any number of formal or informal review points. Typically the team pick up one or more products or user stories and evolve these iteratively until completed. Completion means a product or user story meets the previously agreed acceptance criteria. The team then pick up the next product or user stories and repeat the process. This free-format style relies on consistent business availability to review and provide feedback on an ongoing basis.

Figure 14.5 The DSDM free-format time-box

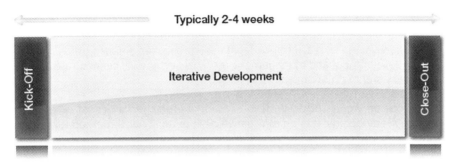

- **Iterative development** – is a process in which the evolving solution, or a part of it, evolves from a high-level concept to something with acknowledged business value. Each cycle of the process is intended to bring the part of the solution being worked on closer to completion and is always a collaborative process, typically involving two or more members of the solution development team. Each cycle should:
  - Be as short as possible, typically taking a day or two, with several cycles happening within a time-box.
  - Be only as formal as it needs to be – in most cases limited to an informal cycle of thought, action and conversation.
  - Involve the appropriate members of the solution development team relevant to the work being done. At its simplest, this could be, for example, a solution developer and a business ambassador working together, or it could need involvement from the whole solution development team, including several business advisors.

14.4 AGILE PROJECT MANAGEMENT

Agile project management (AgilePM; DSDM Consortium, 2014a) is based on the current version of DSDM (see Section 14.3). AgilePM provides a view of DSDM from the point of view of a project manager, managing an Agile project using an appropriate Agile management style i.e. facilitative, rather than command and control. AgilePM focuses on what an Agile project manager needs to consider and the behaviours and mind-set an Agile Project Manager needs to adopt in order to support and enable self-organising teams. The basics of DSDM (see Section 14.3) also form the basis of AgilePM.

AgilePM has also been defined in such a way that it can be used to provide a 'project' wrapper for other Agile approaches. For example, where Scrum is the preferred Agile choice at team level, but where an overarching project framework is still needed. DSDM has also published a pocket book describing a customisation of AgilePM framework customised specifically to meet the needs of a Scrum project.

14.5 KANBAN

The Kanban method (Anderson, 2010) is an approach to continuously improving service delivery that emphasises the smooth, fast flow of work. Organisationally Kanban is used for all creative and knowledge work service delivery and workflows. It has been used in video editing, advertising, recruitment, legal case processes, finance, sales, marketing, community development and management, etc. This section will concentrate on Kanban within delivery and maintenance of IT systems.

Kanban is not an Agile software development method (or process) or a software engineering methodology; it is an alternative path to agility or a method for improving service delivery agility aimed at improving business resilience and fitness for purpose. It's also been described as a method for improving organisational agility as opposed to product development agility with first generation Agile methods.

Kanban does not prescribe specific roles or process steps as it is built on the concept of evolutionary change. Start by understanding how the current software delivery system works. When the current flow of work is visualised and measured, improve it one step at a time. Continue to do this forever.

14.5.1 Six core Kanban practices

The six core practices are;

- Visualise the work;
- Limit work-in-progress (WIP);
- Make policies explicit;
- Measure and manage flow;
- Implement feedback loops;
- Improve collaboratively, evolve experimentally.

These are presented in further detail in the following subsections.

14.5.1.1 Visualise the work, the workflow and business risks

The concept of 'inventory' in a software delivery system is tricky – it is effectively invisible since we are dealing with the flow of ideas. Visualising each step in the value chain from vague idea to released software is a prerequisite for effective management of the end-to-end delivery process. This is normally done on a physical board with Post-It® notes or similar to represent the work (see Figure 14.6). Work flows across the board from left to right.

14.5.1.2 Limit work-in-progress (WIP)

Limiting the amount of work items being worked on at any one time is a counter-intuitive approach to improving the flow of work ('work items' in this context means customer-valued (or requested) work and not tasks). Kanban teams are interested in tracking the flow of value and not the effort expended. Kanban is about managing customer-valued work rather than managing people. The demands of the customer – what they want and when they need it – determine how people organise their work to deliver against these expectations. By limiting the amount of work-in-progress at particular process steps, work items are held upstream until another work item is finished, capacity then becomes available and they can be pulled into the process. A kind of 'one in, one out' policy – similar to that operated by bouncers at busy nightclubs!

Figure 14.6 Typical Kanban board

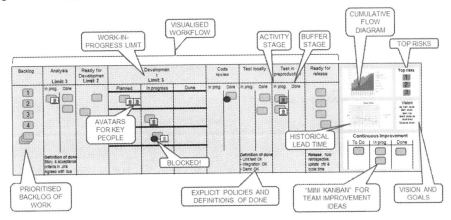

Lowering WIP reduces coordination costs (less to coordinate!), reduces multi-tasking and increases focus. The process becomes more responsive to unplanned external events (e.g. 'we have a new urgent requirement') and process failures (e.g. 'we found in our final testing that the new architecture is not going to work.'). Less WIP also results in reduced lead times (time it takes for work items to flow through the process) since we have a small number of fast flowing items instead of a large number of slow moving items. Average lead time is directly related to WIP according to Little's law (Little and Graves, 2008).

Perhaps less obvious is that gradually lowering the WIP limits drives collaborative improvement of the whole process. Restricting WIP will cause some process steps (those with overcapacity) to be starved of work. This 'pain' prompts the operators and the management of these process steps to investigate what is happening upstream and downstream (seeing as this is conveniently visualised, this should not be too difficult). This typically results in a process redesign or optimisation to improve the flow between these process steps. Setting appropriate WIP levels is somewhat of a 'black art' – set them too high and they have no effect, set them too low and they choke off the flow of work. Experimenting with WIP limits is encouraged, as it is relatively easy to reverse any changes to the WIP limits.

14.5.1.3 Make policies explicit

All management, risk management and process policies that apply to the process must be documented. For example, the team may produce checklists of what needs to have happened in order to consider a specific step in the process as complete or they may document how particular decisions are to be made.

14.5.1.4 Manage flow

Transitions between process steps in the workflow are monitored and measured. This gives a historical picture of the flow of work, lead times etc. Analysing this gives insights into opportunities for improvement and also determines whether any changes previously made have actually resulted in an improvement to the process.

Cumulative flow diagrams (Figure 14.7) are powerful tools for visualising the history of the flow of work. WIP levels on any given date can be read off the vertical scale (see week 3 in Figure 14.7). Less obviously, average lead times can be read off the horizontal scale (2 weeks for work items begun in week 3). The slope of a line in a cumulative flow diagram is the rate at which work is transitioning from one process step to the next – the steeper the line, the greater the rate of transition.

Figure 14.7 Cumulative flow diagram

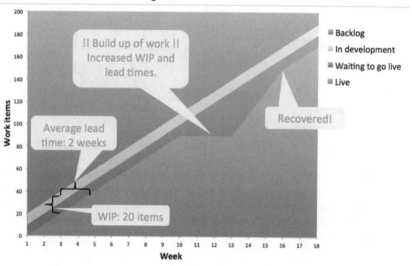

14.5.1.5 Implement feedback loops

Kanban encourages the use of feedback loops at all levels to facilitate learning about the process and about the effect of any changes that have been made to it.

14.5.1.6 Improve collaboratively, evolve experimentally

A significant part of the Kanban method is its emphasis on the creation of a culture to support continuous change. In particular, a 'Kaizen' (Womack, Jones and Roos, 2007) culture in which continuous improvement is seen as everyone's job at all levels within the organisation and all feel empowered to make changes.

14.5.2 Kanban models

Kanban encourages the use of models to identify changes that, if applied, will likely result in an improvement. Common Kanban models include:

- The theory of profound knowledge or the PDCA/PDSA cycle (the most common model; Deming, n.d.).

- The real option theory (Matts, 2013) and related concepts from financial risk management such as market liquidity.

- Sense-making techniques for clustering assignable cause variations are now being synthesised with event-driven risk management from the project management body of knowledge or PMBoK (PMI, 2013).

- The theory of constraints (Goldratt and Cox, 1984).

- Transaction, coordination costs and information arrival rates (and Shannon's information theory) is also used (Shannon, 1948).

14.5.3 Kanban origins

Kanban was adapted from the Lean manufacturing (Liker, 2004) approach of the same name by David J. Anderson in 2007 (Anderson, 2010). As David Anderson himself says: 'What Kanban first and foremost does is serve as a catalyst to introduce Lean ideas into software delivery systems' (Anderson, 2010).

The word 'Kanban' itself is a Japanese word used originally by Toyota to mean 'signal card'. The 'signal card' is physical card in the Toyota plant that signalled when to pull more inventory from a supply step or storage location.

14.5.4 Kanban and Scrum

Kanban is often contrasted with Scrum (see Section 14.2).

Table 14.1 Kanban/Scrum comparison

Kanban	Scrum
An approach to improving service delivery using evolutionary improvement.	An approach to complex product development.
No roles or processes defined.	Standard roles and processes clearly defined.
Evolutionary. Start with what already exists and iterate. Respect what is.	Revolutionary. Do it like Scrum says. Doesn't matter what has gone before.
WIP limited by a 'pull' system based on work orders or requirements. Limit the work and let time vary.	WIP never exceeds the amount that can be completed by the team in a sprint. Limit the time and vary the work to fit the defined time period.

Organisations sometimes combine Kanban and Scrum, although either framework will work perfectly well on its own. There are several ways this can be valuable:

- 'Scrumban' (Ladas, 2009) (Kanban within a Scrum team) – Scrum teams use Kanban to manage the work they do within a sprint.

- Enterprise (Kanban above Scrum team) – Scrum teams may contribute to larger programmes of work involving multiple teams. These larger programmes apply Kanban at a higher level to manage some or all of the work. The portfolio level in SAFe (See Section 14.8) is a good example of this.

- End-to-end process (Kanban upstream and downstream of Scrum team) – A full Scrum implementation implies there is no downstream or upstream activity outside the team – everybody who is required to deliver value should be within the boundaries of the team. In practice, teams rarely start like this. Kanban can be helpful in visualising and addressing this situation both upstream (requirements analysis, architectural design, etc.) and downstream (release management, integration testing, documentation, etc.) of the Scrum team.

- Adopt Kanban for work that does not fit Scrum – Many teams work on items that are unsuitable for Scrum. Some will not be able to create a 'useable and potentially shippable product increment' within a month (e.g. teams working on large legacy software systems with lots of manual tests). Other teams will experience so much requirement volatility that they are unable to make a plan for a whole sprint (e.g. reactive support work). Yet other teams do not have a 'product increment' as their primary output (e.g. DevOps team, enterprise architect team, senior management team, etc.). In these contexts, Kanban without Scrum is a good fit.

- Some Agile teams adopt Kanban without Scrum because they are unable to gain sufficient internal alignment to implement the major organisational and procedural changes required for effective Scrum.

14.6 LEAN SOFTWARE DEVELOPMENT

Lean software development originated in 2003 with the work of Mary and Tom Poppendieck (Poppendieck, 2003). It is based on adapting ideas from Lean manufacturing to a software development context. This approach has been enthusiastically embraced by the Agile community. Lean principles often provide an explanation for why many Agile practices work, based on proven evidence and also provide a framework for improving and scaling an Agile approach. In fact, the boundary between Lean and Agile has become blurred over time.

The original Lean manufacturing approach was created by Toyota (Womack, Jones and Roos, 2007) and focuses on the elimination of non-value-adding activities (waste) in the manufacturing process. Some adjustment to this approach is needed as the nature of software development is fundamentally different from manufacturing in two key ways:

- Manufacturing is a repetitive process. Software development is not repetitive as both requirements and solutions are unique. They also typically build on previous requirements/solutions. This places greater emphasis on learning – both about how to build a solution and whether it is valuable or not. In particular, learning is achieved through fast feedback.

- Both manufacturing and software development processes are able to influence the cost and quality of their respective outputs, but only software development can make a significant difference to the value of the product in the customer's eyes by discovering valuable stories that were not thought of up front and avoiding developing stories that have no value. In fact, a Lean software approach suggests that this is likely the biggest win in terms of improvement efforts. As such, the original Lean manufacturing focus of elimination of non-value (waste) is typically recast to the broader 'maximise value' in order to include the possibility of value creation.

The full Lean software development approach consists of seven core principles (Poppendieck and Poppendieck, 2007), supported by 22 tools. Mary Poppendieck boils down Lean software development as it applies to a team (Poppendieck, 2014) to five key questions:

- Is the team a whole team – composed of everyone necessary to deliver value to the ultimate customer?

- Does everyone on the team understand what customers really value?

- Is the team focused on delivering small increments of real value to end customers?

- Does the team reliably and repeatedly deliver on its promises?

- Is there a leader who understands and cares deeply about the customers and their problems and a leader who understands and cares deeply about the technical integrity of the product?

14.6.1 Seven Lean software development principles

14.6.1.1 Principle 1: Eliminate waste

The three biggest wastes in software development are:

- **Extra stories** A process is needed for developing just those 20 per cent of the stories that give 80 per cent of the value.

- **Churn** If there is requirements churn, specification is happening early. If there are test and fix cycles, the testing is too late.

- **Crossing boundaries** Organisational boundaries can increase costs by 25 per cent or more. They create buffers that slow down response time and interfere with communication.

14.6.1.2 Principle 2: Build in quality

If defects are routinely found in the verification process, the development process is defective.

- Mistake-proofing code with test-driven development. Writing executable specifications instead of requirements.
- Not building legacy code. Legacy code is code that lacks automated unit and acceptance tests.

14.6.1.3 Principle 3: Create knowledge

Planning is useful, learning essential.

- Use the scientific method. Teach teams to establish hypotheses, conduct many rapid experiments, create concise documentation and implement the best alternative.
- Standards exist to be challenged and improved. Embody the current best-known practices in standards that are always followed while actively encouraging everyone to challenge and change these standards.
- Predictable performance is driven by feedback. Don't guess about the future and call it a plan; use feedback based on reality to develop the capacity to rapidly respond to the future as it unfolds.

14.6.1.4 Principle 4: Defer commitment

Abolish the idea that it is a good idea to start development with a complete specification.

- Break dependencies. System architecture should support the addition of any PBI at any time.
- Maintain options. Think of code as an experiment – make it change-tolerant.
- Schedule irreversible decisions at the last responsible moment. Learn as much as possible before making irreversible decisions

14.6.1.5 Principle 5: Deliver fast

Queues (points in a delivery process where the process stops whilst waiting for something, like a sign-off) are buffers between organisations that slow things down.

- Rapid delivery, high quality and low cost are fully compatible. Companies that compete on the basis of efficient, rapid, value chains have significant cost advantage, deliver superior quality, and are most attuned to their customers' needs.
- Queuing theory applies to development, not just servers. Focusing on utilisation creates traffic jams that actually reduce utilisation. Drive down cycle time with small batches and restrict work-in-progress where required.
- Limit work to capacity. Establish a reliable, repeatable velocity with iterative development. Aggressively limit the size of work in progress to optimise delivery flow.

14.6.1.6 Principle 6: Respect people

Engaged, thinking people provide the most sustainable competitive advantage.

- Teams thrive on pride, commitment, trust and applause. What makes a team? Members are mutually committed to achieving a common goal.

- Provide effective leadership. Effective teams have effective leaders who bring out the best in the team.

- Respect partners. Allegiance to the joint venture must never create a conflict of interest, the venture must be beneficial to both parties.

14.6.1.7 Principle 7: Optimise the whole

Brilliant products emerge from a unique combination of opportunity and technology.

- Focus on the entire value stream. From concept to cash. From customer request to deployed software, focus on the whole delivery process from start to end, not just one part of the process.

- Deliver a complete product. Develop a complete product, not just software; this may include documentation, business change, etc. Complete products are built by complete teams.

- Measure up. Measure process capability with cycle time. Measure team performance with delivered business value. Measure customer satisfaction with a net promoter score (a customer loyalty metric; Reichheld 2003).

14.6.2 Twenty-two Lean software development tools

The seven core principles are supported by 22 tools.

- **Seeing waste** Some wastes are obvious, defects for example. Some are more subtle: extra stories, waiting, task switching.

- **Value stream mapping** Map out the flow of a requirement from idea to rollout. This helps identify queues, waiting, excessive hand-offs, non-value-add steps and so on.

- **Feedback** Increase the speed and the quality of feedback at many levels to improve process quality.

- **Iterations** Deliver early and often to get feedback on the product and its value.

- **Synchronisation** Integrate software frequently to avoid surprises and rework.

- **Set-based development** Work on multiple options or let the solution emerge.

- **Options thinking** Keeping options open has a value – delay decisions if possible until more information is available.

- **Last responsible moment** This is the point at which, if a decision is delayed any further, an important option will be eliminated. Delay the decision no further than this.

- **Making decisions** Devolve decision to the team level as far as possible and be guided by simple decision-making rules (e.g. agree rules that define a clear prioritisation method for stories in the backlog with all stakeholders).

- **Pull systems** Allow teams to pull in work when they have capacity. Do not push the work to them as this increases the amount of work-in-progress without increasing throughput.

- **Queuing theory** Identify, measure and reduce queues of partially complete work in the development process. There are numerous ways to do this, however, measuring cost of delay is a good start point (see Section 10.1).

- **Cost of delay** Build an economic model that puts a price on speed of delivery so it can be traded off against other factors like risk, cost and so on.

- **Self-determination** Allow teams to decide how they organise their own work.

- **Motivation** Team motivation comes from an achievable purpose, access to the customer and a freedom to make their own commitments in an environment in which mistakes are opportunities to learn.

- **Leadership** Most successful initiatives have a product champion and a master developer who care passionately about the customer and the integrity of the product respectively.

- **Expertise** Share expertise and enforce standards by the Agile lead (see Section 6.3) facilitating the team to become self-organising and to work in a collaborative way.

- **Perceived integrity** Align all activities to customer value so that it is clear why things are happening.

- **Conceptual integrity** Ensure that components/interfaces of the product work together as a smooth cohesive whole.

- **Refactoring** Essential to maintain the health of the product as not everything can be foreseen up front at design time.

- **Testing** Automate testing to speed up the feedback loop.

- **Measurements** Make problems and progress visible.

- **Contracts** Avoid fixing scope up front in a contract.

14.7 LEAN START-UP

The Lean start-up approach began with a book of the same name (Ries, 2011) and is now a worldwide movement. It is rooted in case studies and the experiences of its creator, Eric Ries. Note that the name can be misleading – running your own company in a Silicon Valley garage is not required to be considered a start-up! In fact, 'anybody who is developing a new product ... under conditions of extreme uncertainty is a start-up' (Ries, 2011: 27). Entrepreneurs are everywhere.

When used in an Agile approach, it is most useful to the product management of brand new products. Lean start-up is not about executing a business model (existing companies do this), but to find a business model. A business model has to answer the following questions:

- How do customers discover the product?

- How do customers get value from the product?

- How is sufficient revenue generated by this for the company to make a profit?

It has been observed that most successful start-ups go from failure to failure before finding a business model that works. The experiments are a series of build–measure–learn feedback loops (see Figure 14.8). An entrepreneur starts with an idea for a business model. They then build a product (or part of a product), which is then put in front of real customers and the results are measured. Learning from these measurements then generates further ideas about how they adjust the business model.

Figure 14.8 The build–measure–learn feedback loop

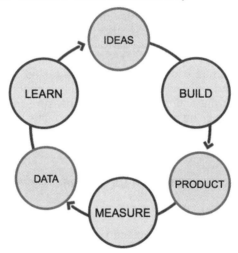

The entrepreneur's role is to maximise the chance of finding a successful business model before running out of funding. This is done by making build–measure–learn loops quick, cheap and effective. Managing this process is what entrepreneurship is all about and the unit of progress is learning.

At the start of the build–measure–learn loop, the entrepreneur has a number of 'leap-of-faith assumptions', which need to be tested. These cover at least:

- **Value hypothesis** Who will see value in the new product or service?

- **Growth hypothesis** How will customers discover the new product or service?

A business model canvas (Blank, 2013) is a common format used to capture on one page all the hypotheses that need testing. It may contain (non-exhaustive list):

- Key partners (suppliers, delivery partners, who does what).

- Key tasks (to get to start-up).

- Key resources and people (equipment, offices, people etc. required).

- Value proposition and MMFS(s) (why should customers buy? Minimum Marketable Feature Set, services/products).

- Finding customers (how to attract customers – social media/campaigns?).

- Market segments (who are being targeted and for what reason(s)?).

- Channels to market (how will we get the right message to those we are targeting?).

- Key costs (over basic timeline).

- Key revenues (over basic timeline).

Given the extreme uncertainty in these hypotheses, the value of getting customer feedback about them far outweighs the benefits of keeping this new product development activity secret from the competition. Entrepreneurs must get out of the building and interact with customers to gauge their reactions – it is the only way to validate their learning.

Hypotheses need to be small enough so they can be tested quickly and the metrics resulting from an experiment need to be actionable. It is important to avoid so-called vanity metrics which look interesting but don't really measure anything that can confirm or deny the hypotheses (e.g. 'number of page views on site' looks good, however, the page may be alienating people or page creating views costs too much).

Example hypotheses from Votizen, a US start-up

Product Concept:

Social network of verified voters, a place where people passionate about civic causes can interact.

Hypotheses:

- Customers are interested enough to sign up [Registration].

- Votizen can verify them as registered voters [Activation].

- Verified voters engage with the network over time [Retention].

- Engaged customers tell their friends about the service [Referral].

Once the hypotheses are identified, Lean start-up recommends applying Lean and Agile development practices to create the minimum viable product (MVP). The MVP is the simplest version of the product that enables a full turn of the build–measure–learn loop.

Once an experiment is run, the moment comes for a decision. Pivot or persevere – i.e. pivot to a different set of hypotheses or persevere and run further experiments tuning the existing product? Pivoting can take many forms: change of customers segment, channel, zooming in on fewer stories, addressing an adjacent customer need that has just been uncovered and so on.

14.8 SCALED AGILE FRAMEWORK (SAFE)

Authors' note: Scaling Agile is a topic that causes much discussion in the Agile community as of 2014. Most of the frameworks described in Part 4 of this book can be scaled on their own. However, the majority of them do not (purposefully, because they are non-prescriptive frameworks) explain how they are scaled. There are also many other frameworks specifically focused on scaling Agile; examples are LESS (Large Scale Scrum; Larman and Vodde, 2013) and DAD (Disciplined Agile Delivery; Ambler and Lines, 2012). The authors think that 'SAFe' is currently the most fully featured, discussed and implemented Agile scaling framework, which is why we have included it in this book.

This section describes SAFe version 3.0.

The Scaled Agile Framework (SAFe) (Leffingwell, 2011–14) is a scaled approach to Agile adoption. Officially launched in 2012, it draws on the experiences of its creator, Dean Leffingwell, and his co-collaborators as to 'effective practices that worked for us' when they found Scrum (see Section 14.2) and eXtreme Programming (see Section 14.1) insufficient in addressing the problems faced by large software organisations.

SAFe is a mix of original work and a container for several existing Agile approaches. The SAFe framework provides:

- A process model that covers the highest and the lowest level in the enterprise. Of particular importance is:
  - A mid-level planning cycle (the program increment, or PI) every 4–6 sprints that covers the activities of 5–12 Scrum teams (an Agile program).
  - Funding of these stable long-term programs, which are aligned to a flow of value to the customer (a value stream).
- Associated Agile values and practices. Many of these practices summarise or simply refer to other Lean or Agile approaches. SAFe endorses or makes reference to: Scrum (see Section 14.2), eXtreme Programming (see Section 14.1), Kanban (see Section 14.5), Lean thinking and Lean product development flow (see Section 14.6), and the Agile Manifesto (see Section 1.2).
- Four core values: code quality, alignment, program execution and transparency.

14.8.1 SAFe process model

SAFe is organised around three layers:

- Teams, who adopt Scrum (or Scrumban) and eXtreme Programming.

- Programs, each of which contains 5–12 teams working towards a common goal.
- Portfolio for funding and coordinating programs.

14.8.1.1 Teams

Figure 14.9 shows that SAFe ScrumXP Teams (Agile teams) power SAFe development and use Scrum (or Scrumban) and eXtreme Programming (XP) as the basis of their work (Leffingwell, 2011–14). There are some adjustments to be made to these standard Agile frameworks, including an understanding of the team's roles in the program, and an emphasis on flow and limiting work-in-progess.

14.8.1.2 Program

In Figure 14.10 the 'Agile release train' (also known as an Agile program) is the primary organisational, operational and value delivery construct. Five to twelve SAFe scrumXP teams form each Agile release train in a value stream. This team-of-teams operates on a planning cycle (program increment) of 8 to 12 weeks.

SAFe describes a 'develop on cadence, release on demand' approach. The development cadence is used to help manage the intrinsic variability of research and development. Releasing occurs on demand, either synchronously or asynchronously with the PI cycle. SAFe makes no recommendations as to release frequency, and leaves that to the discretion of the individual release trains.

SAFe defines nine roles at the program level:

- **Product management** Prioritises program backlog. Owns and communicates product vision and roadmap.
- **Release train engineer** Drives program level continuous improvement. Facilitates PI release (a kind of 'ScrumMaster' (see Section 14.2) for the Agile release train).
- **Business owner** Senior management responsible (ultimately) for value delivery. Participates in release planning and release inspect and adapt (see below).
- **System architect** Helps break down system-level stories. Liaises with enterprise architecture.
- **User Interface team** (UX) Creates a consistent user experience.
- **System team** Provides process and tools to integrate and evaluate early and often. Enables system-level continuous integration.
- **DevOps** Characterises the skills needed by the programs to build and improve a rapid deployment pipeline.
- **Release management** Synchronises releases with other programs and stakeholders.
- **Shared resources** Provide assistance in specialist areas not normally found in the teams.

Figure 14.9 SAFe team level

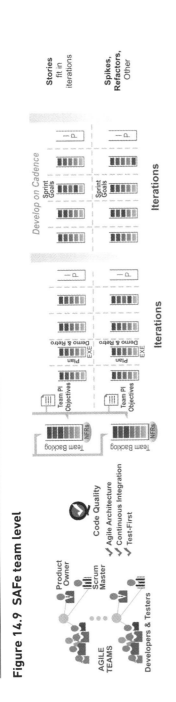

Figure 14.10 SAFe program level

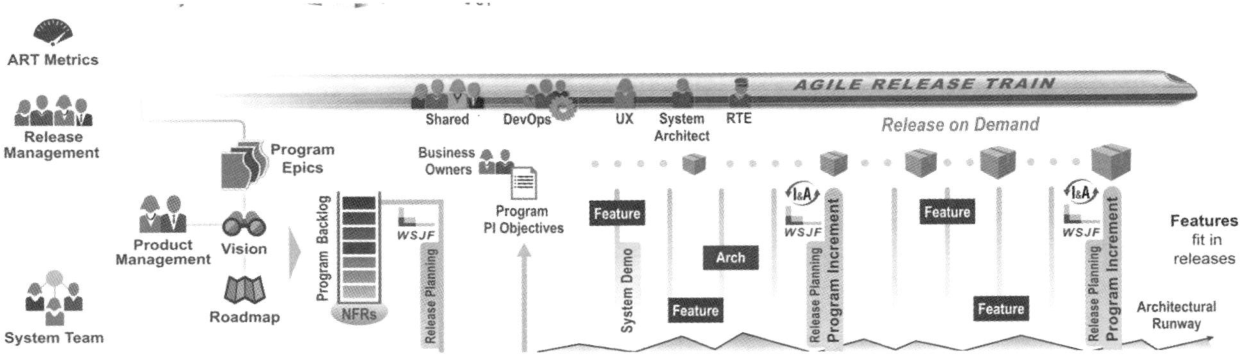

Each program increment (PI) begins with a 2 day 'all hands' planning session, which everybody in the program attends. It is at this event that the overall PI objectives are identified along with team-specific PI objectives, and a release plan is made to achieve them over the next four to six sprints. A vote of confidence/commitment in the release plan that has been defined is also held.

Once the train is underway, coordination between teams is achieved, in part, through a standard Scrum-of-Scrums meeting (see Section 14.2), facilitated by the release train engineer. A system-level demonstration is given to relevant stakeholders at the end of each sprint to review progress. The final sprint in the release plan cycle may be an innovation and planning (IP) sprint. This provides time for:

- Innovation, exploration and out-of-the-box thinking; and
- Planning the next PSI release.

Scheduling IP sprints at the end of each program increment can also serve as a schedule buffer if planned development overruns.

An inspect and adapt workshop (I&A) is at the end of each program increment. The I&A is to a SAFe program as a sprint review and retrospective are to a Scrum team (see Section 14.2), that is, an opportunity for reflection and adjustment, but at the level of the program, where most of the larger, systemic impediments occur.

14.8.1.3 Portfolio

The SAFe portfolio layer (see Figure 14.11) is responsible for:

- Coordinating larger initiatives (epics) that require implementation across multiple release trains. These are managed in the portfolio backlog.
- Funding of Agile release trains.

The portfolio backlog contains epics that cross multiple release trains. These can be either customer-facing (business epics) or technology (architectural epics) initiatives. To get into the backlog, initiatives need analysis and approval. The work at this level is managed using a Kanban system (See Section 14.5).

Every Agile release train is aligned within a value stream (i.e. a significant flow of value to the customer) and is funded by an associated budget. Budgets are determined by the current business context and the evolving portfolio strategic themes.

Roles in the SAFe portfolio layer are more loosely defined than they are in the other two layers of SAFe. They include program portfolio management, enterprise architecture and epic owners.

14.8.2 SAFe Agile architecture

SAFe contends that **emergent architecture** (design grown incrementally), while effective for the team's local concerns, is not sufficient at scale. Some intentional architecture is required (design done up front). SAFe aims to provide just enough of this up-front

Figure 14.11 SAFe portfolio level

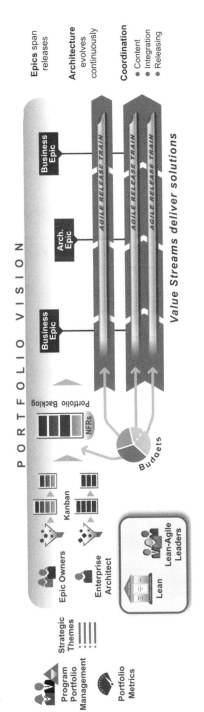

163

architecture just in time to enable teams to progress effectively. Architectural features that are built just in time to enable business features result in software code known as the architectural runway.

Non-functional requirements (reliability, scalability, maintainability and so on) are key architectural concerns in SAFe. They are most typically associated with program-level backlogs, either as a single backlog item or a constraint on all backlog items (e.g., 'web pages load in under 2 s').

REFERENCES

Adkins, L. (2010) *Coaching Agile teams: a companion for ScrumMasters, Agile coaches, and project managers in transition.* Upper Saddle River, New Jersey: Addison-Wesley.

Adzic, G. (2010) *Specification by example.* New York: Manning.

Agile Manifesto (2001) Available online at http://agilemanifesto.org/ [accessed 5 December, 2014].

Ambler, S. and Lines, M. (2012) *Disciplined Agile delivery: a practitioner's guide to Agile software delivery in the enterprise.* Indianapolis: IBM Press.

Ambler, S. (2001–14) 'Communication on Agile software teams'. Available online at www.agilemodeling.com/essays/communication.htm [accessed 21 July, 2014].

Anderson, D. J. (2010) *Kanban – successful evolutionary change for your information technology business.* Blue Hole Press.

Axelos (2014), 'PRINCE2 Principles'. Available online at https://www.axelos.com/what-is-prince2 [accessed 9 December, 2014].

Beck, K. (2002) *Test Driven Development: by example.* Boston, MA: Addison-Wesley.

Beck, K. (2004) *Extreme programming explained: embrace change*, 2nd Edn. Boston, MA: Addison-Wesley.

Blank, S. (2013) 'Why the Lean start-up changes everything'. *Harvard Business Review.*

Boehm, B. (1981) *Software engineering economics.* Upper Saddle River, NJ: Prentice-Hall.

Boehm, B. (1986) 'A spiral model of software development and enhancement'. ACM SIGSOFT Software Engineering Notes, 11 (4), 14–24.

Boyd, J. (n.d.) 'OODA Loop'. Available online at www.mindtools.com/pages/article/newTED_78.htm [accessed 16 June, 2014].

Brooks, F. (1995) *Mythical man-month.* Boston, MA: Addison-Wesley.

Bryner, J. (2007, July 1) 'Humans learn from making mistakes'. Available online at www.livescience.com/7312-study-reveals-learn-mistakes.html [accessed 16 June, 2014].

Bryson, J. M. (2013) 'What to do when stakeholders matter'. Available online at http://cep.lse.ac.uk/seminarpapers/10-02-03-bry.pdf [accessed 16 June, 2014].

Carmel, E. and Tija, P. (2005) *Offshoring information technology: sourcing and outsourcing to a global workforce.* New York: Cambridge University Press.

Chapman, S. (1909) 'Theory of the hours of labour'. *The Economic Journal.*

CMMi. (n.d.) 'Capability maturity model Integration'. Available online at http://whatis.cmmiinstitute.com [accessed 16 June, 2014].

Cockburn, A. (2004) *Crystal clear: a human powered methodology for small teams.* Boston, MA: Addison-Wesley.

Cohn, M. (2005) *Agile estimating and planning.* Upper Saddle River, NJ: Prentice Hall.

Cohn, M. (n.d.) 'It's effort not complexity'. Available online at www.mountaingoatsoftware.com/blog/its-effort-not-complexity [accessed 22 July, 2014].

Covey, S. R. (1989) *The seven habits of highly effective people.* New York: Free Press.

Crispin, L. and Gregory, J. (2009) *Agile testing.* Boston, MA: Addison-Wesley.

Deming, E. (n.d.) 'PDSA Cycle'. Available online at https://deming.org/theman/theories/pdsacycle [accessed 16 June, 2014].

Deutsch, M. (1958) 'Trust and suspicion'. *Journal of Conflict Resolution,* 265–79.

Drucker, P. F. (2001) *Management challenges for the 21st century.* New York: HarperBusiness.

DSDM Consortium. (2014a) *Agile project management.* Available online at www.apmg-international.com/en/qualifications/agile-pm/agile-pm.aspx [accessed 25 August, 2014].

DSDM Consortium. (2014b) *DSDM Consortium.* Available online at www.dsdm.org [accessed 11 August, 2014].

Dweck, C. S. (2012) *The Agile mindset: how you can fulfill your potential.* London: Robinson.

Evans P. A. L. (2000) 'The dualistic leader: thriving on paradoxes', In Chowdhury, S. (ed.), *Management 21C: someday we'll all manage this way.* Financial Times/Prentice Hall.

Feynman, R. (1974) 'Cargo cult science'. Available online at www.neurotheory.columbia.edu/~ken/cargo_cult.html [accessed 30 June, 2014].

Fowler, M., Beck, K., Brant, J., Opdyke, W. and Robert, D. (1999) *Refactoring: improving the design of existing code.* Boston, MA: Addison Wesley.

Fowler, M. (2011) 'Specification by example'. Available online at http://martinfowler.com/bliki/SpecificationByExample.html [accessed 16 June, 2014].

Fowler, M. (n.d.) 'Continuous integration'. Available online at http://martinfowler.com/articles/continuousIntegration.html [accessed 21 December, 2014].

Gilb, T. (n.d.) 'Evo makes project failure structurally impossible!' Available online at www.gilb.com/Project-Management [accessed 21 December, 2014].

Goldratt, E. M. and Cox, J. (1984) *The goal: a process of ongoing improvement.* Great Barrington, MA: The North River Press.

Greenleaf, R. (1970) 'What is servant-leadership'. Available online at https://greenleaf.org/what-is-servant-leadership/ [accessed 21 December, 2014].

Grenning, J. (2002) 'Planning poker'. Available online at http://renaissancesoftware.net/papers/14-papers/44-planing-poker.html [accessed 22 July, 2014].

Herzberg, F. (1968) 'One more time: how do you motivate employees'. *Harvard Business Review.*

Hewitt, R. T. (2013, April 3) 'Introducing the three amigos'. Available online at https://www.scrumalliance.org/community/articles/2013/2013-april/introducing-the-three-amigos [accessed 25 August, 2014].

Hickman, K. (2014) 'Franco-Prussian War: Field Marshal Helmuth von Moltke the Elder'. Available online at http://militaryhistory.about.com/od/1800sarmybiographies/p/vonmoltke.htm [accessed 5 December, 2014].

Hofstede, G. (1994) *Cultures and organisations: software of the mind: intercultural cooperation and its importance for surviva.* London: HarperCollins.

Holloway Consulting. (2014) 'Scheduled overtime effect on construction projects'. Available online at www.hcgexperts.com/scheduled-overtime-effect-on-construction-projects.php [accessed 5 December, 2014].

IBMRational. (n.d.) 'Rational Unified Process'. Available online at www.01.ibm.com/software/rational/rup/ [accessed 16 June, 2014].

James, G. (2012) 'Stop working more than 40 hours / week'. Available online at www.inc.com/geoffrey-james/stop-working-more-than-40-hours-a-week.html [accessed 14 July, 2014].

Johnson, J. (2002) 'Features used in a typical system delivery'. *Chaos Report.* The Standish Group.

Kerzner, H. (2013) *Project management metrics, KPIs and dashboards: a guide to measuring and monitoring project performance,* 2nd Edn. Wiley.

Koch, R. (1998) *The 80/20 principle.* London: Random House.

Kotter, J. (1996) *Leading change.* Harvard: Harvard Business School Press.

Ladas, C. (2009) *Essays on Kanban systems for Lean software development.* WA: Modus Cooperandi Lean.

Larman, C. (2003) *Agile and Iterative Development: A Manager's Guide.* Upper Saddle River, NJ: Addison-Wesley.

Larman, C. and Vodde, B. (2013, June) 'LeSS: Large Scaled Scrum'. Available online at www.crosstalkonline.org/storage/issue-archives/2013/201305/201305-Larman.pdf [accessed 22 July, 2014].

Leffingwell, D. (2011–14) 'Scaled Agile Framework (SAFe)'. Available online at www.scaledagileframework.com [accessed 21 May, 2014].

Lencioni, P. (2002) *The five dysfunctions of a team.* San Francisco: Jossey-Bass.

Liker, J. K. (2004) *The Toyota way: 14 management principles from the world's greatest manufacturer.* New York: McGraw-Hill.

Little, J. D. C. and Graves, S. C. (2008) 'Little's Law'. In D. Chhajed and T.J. Lowe (eds), *Building intuition: insights from basic operations management models and principles.* New York: Springer.

Mah, M. and Lunt, M. (2008) 'How Agile projects measure up and what this means to you'. Available online at Cutter Consortium: www.qsm-europe.com/fjc_documents/mah-howagilemeasuresup.1.pdf [accessed 5 Aug, 2014].

Martin, J. (n.d.) 'RAD/JAD'. Available online at http://en.wikipedia.org/wiki/Rapid_application_development [accessed 21 December, 2014].

Martin, R. (2000) 'Principles and patterns'. Available online at www.objectmentor.com/resources/articles/Principles_and_Patterns.pdf [accessed 16 July, 2014].

Maslow, A. H. (1943) 'A theory of human motivation'. *Psychological Review*, 50, 370–96. Available online at http://psychclassics.yorku.ca/Maslow/motivation.htm, [accessed 21 December, 2014].

Maslow, A. H. (1970a) *Motivation and personality.* New York: Harper and Row.

Maslow, A. H. (1970b) *Religions, values and peak experiences.* New York: Penguin.

Matts, C. (2007) 'Real Options Enhance Agility'. Available online at www.infoq.com/articles/real-options-enhance-agility [accessed 22 July, 2014].

Matts, C. (2013) 'Chris matts on BDD, feature injection and commitment'. www.infoq.com/interviews/matts-commitment-bdd. (InfoQ, Interviewer).

McBreen, P. (2002) *Software craftsmanship: The New Imperative.* Boston, MA: Addison Wesley.

McGregor, D. and Gershenfeld, J. (2006) *The human side of enterprise.* New York: McGraw-Hill.

McGregor, D. (1960) *The human side of enterprise.* New York: McGraw-Hill.

Myers, B. (2002) *Principles of corporate finance,* 7th Edn. New York: McGraw-Hill.

North, D. (2006) 'Introducing BDD'. Available online at dannorth.net: http://dannorth.net/introducing-bdd/ [accessed 21 December, 2014].

Orsburn, J. D. (1990) *Self-directed work teams: the new American challenge.* Homewood, Il: Business One Irwin.

Oxford Dictionary. (2014) 'Parkinson's law'. Available online at www.oxforddictionaries.com/definition/english/Parkinson's-law [accessed 22 July, 2014].

Pink, D. (2009) *Drive: the surprising truth about what motivates us.* New York: Penguin.

Plant, R. (1989) *The organisational iceberg: managing change and making it stick.* London, UK: Fontana/Collins.

PMI. (2013) *A guide to the project management body of knowledge: PMBOK guide,* 5th Edn. Newton Square, PA: Project Management Institute.

Polgar, L. (1989) *Bring up genius.* Budapest: Kossuth Kiado.

Poppendieck, T. (2003) *Lean software development: an Agile toolkit.* Boston, MA: Addison-Wesley.

Poppendieck, M. (2014) 'Lean Magazine'. Available online at http://leanmagazine.net/lean/lean-development-boil-down-to/ [accessed 21 December, 2014].

Poppendieck, M. and Poppendieck, T. (2007) *Implementing Lean Software Development: from concept to cash.* Upper Saddle River, NJ: Addison-Wesley.

PRINCE2. (2011) *PRINCE2.* London: AXELOS Limited.

Pugh, K. (2011) *Lean–Agile acceptance test-driven development: better software through collaboration.* Boston, MA: Addison-Wesley.

Reichheld, F. (2003) 'The one number you need to grow'. Available online at http://hbr.org/2003/12/the-one-number-you-need-to-grow/ [accessed 16 June, 2014].

Reinertsen, D. (2009) *The principles of product development flow: second generation Lean product developmen.* Redondo Beach, CA: Celeritas.

Ries, E. (2011) *The Lean startup: how today's entrepreneurs use continuous innovation to create radically successful businesses.* New York: Crown Business.

Rising, L. (n.d.) www.agilealliance.org. Available online at www.agilealliance.org/resources/learning-center/keynote-the-power-of-an-agile-mindset/ [accessed 21 December, 2014].

Royce, W. (1987[1970]) 'Managing the development of large software systems'. *Proceedings of the Ninth International Conference on Software Engineering,* March, 328–38. Available online at www.cs.umd.edu/class/spring2003/cmsc838p/Process/waterfall.pdf [accessed 16 June, 2014].

Rubin, K. (2013) *Essential Scrum: A practical guide to the most popular Agile process.* Upper Saddle River, New Jersey: Addison-Wesley.

Sahota, Michael (2012) 'An Agile adoption and transformation survival guide: working with organizational culture'. Available online at www.infoq.com/minibooks/agile-adoption-transformation [accessed 19 January, 2015].

Schneider, W. E. (1999) *The reengineering alternative: a plan for making your current culture work.* New York: McGraw-Hill.

Schwaber, K. (2004) *Agile project management with Scrum.* Redmond, Washington: Microsoft Press.

Schwaber, K. and Beedle, M. (2001) *Agile software development with Scrum.* Upper Saddle River, NJ: Prentice Hall.

Schwaber, K. and Sutherland, J. (n.d.) 'The Scrum guide'. Available online at www.scrum.org [accessed 21 December, 2014].

Shannon, C. (1948) 'A mathematical theory of communication'. *Bell System Technical Journal,* 27, 379–423 and 623–56.

Six Sigma (2006) 'Motorola University Six Sigma Dictionary'. Available online at https://web.archive.org/web/20060128110005/www.motorola.com/content/0,,3074-5804,00.html#ss. Archived from the original on 28 January, 2006 [accessed 14 December, 2014].

Snowdon, D. and Boone, M. (2007) 'A leader's framework for decision making'. *Harvard Business Review (Nov).* Available online at http://hbr.org/2007/11/a-leaders-framework-for-decision-making/ [accessed 16 June, 2014].

Software Craftsmanship (2009) 'Software craftsmanship'. Available online at http://manifesto.softwarecraftsmanship.org/ [accessed 1 December, 2014].

Spayd, Michael (2011) 'How to make your culture work with Agile, Kanban & Software Craftsmanship'. Available online at www.methodsandtools.com/archive/agileculture.php [accessed 19 January, 2015].

Stacey, R. (1996) *Complexity and creativity in organisations.* San Francisco, CA: Berrett Kochler.

Standish (2002) 'The Chaos Manifesto'. Available online at www.standishgroup.com/ [accessed 14 December, 2014].

Sutherland, J. and Schwaber, K. (2013) *The Scrum guide: the definitive guide to Scrum: the rules of the game.* Available online at www.academia.edu/8370895/The_Scrum_Guide_The_Definitive_Guide_to_Scrum_The_Rules_of_the_Game [accessed 14 December, 2014].

Sutherland, J.V., Patel, D., Casanave, C., Miller, J. and Hollowell, G. (1995) *OOPSLA '95 workshop proceedings,*16 October 1995, Austin, Texas, Volume 1. Austin: Springer.

Syed, M. (2011) *Bounce: Beckham, Serena, Mozart and the science of success.* London: Fourth Estate.

Tabaka, J. (2006) *Collaboration explained.* Upper Saddle River, NJ: Addison-Wesley.

Takeuchi, H. and Nonaka, I. (1986) 'New new product development game'. Available online at Harvard Business Review: http://hbr.org/1986/01/the-new-new-product-development-game/ar/1 [accessed 14 December, 2014].

Tuckman, B. (1965) 'Developmental sequence in small groups'. *Psychological Bulletin 63*, 384–99.

VersionOne. (n.d.) '2013 State of Agile Survey'. Available online at http://stateofagile.com/8th-annual-state-of-agile-form/ [accessed 14 July, 2014].

Verzuh, E. (2008) *The Fast Forward MBA in Project Management,* 3rd Edn. Hoboken, NJ: John Wiley & Sons.

Wahba, M. and Bridwell, L. (1976) 'Maslow reconsidered: A review of research on the need hierarchy theory'. *Organisational Behavior and Human Performance*, 212–40.

Wells, D. (2009) 'Set a sustainable, measurable, predictable pace'. Available online at www.extremeprogramming.org/rules/overtime.htm [accessed 27 May, 2014].

Womack, J., Jones, D. and Roos D. (2007) *The machine that changed the world.* London: Simon and Schuster.

Zajonc, R. (1968) 'Attitudinal effects of mere exposure'. *Journal of Personality and Social Psychology*, 9 (2), 1–27.

RECOMMENDED FURTHER READING OR 'WHAT'S ON OUR OFFICE BOOKSHELF'

Agile Alliance The Agile Alliance Guide to Agile Practices http://guide.Agilealliance.org/

Anderson, David J. (2012) *Lessons in Agile management: on the road to Kanban.* Sequim WA: Blue Hole Press.

Astels, D., Miller, G. and Novak, M. (2002) *A practical guide to eXtreme programming.* Upper Saddle River, NJ: Prentice Hall.

Cohn, Mike (2009) *Succeeding with Agile.* Upper Saddle River, NJ: Addison-Wesley.

Cohn, Mike (2009) *User stories applied.* New Jersey: Addison-Wesley

Davies, Rachel and Sedley, Liz (2009) *Agile coaching.* US: Pragmatic Programmers.

Denning, S. (2010) *The leader's guide to radical management: reinventing the workplace for the 21st century.* San Francisco, CA: Jossey-Bass.

Derby, Ester and Larsen, Diana (2006) *Agile retrospectives: making good teams great.* Dallas, TX: The Pragmatic Bookshelf.

Feathers, Michael (2004) *Working effectively with legacy code.* New Jersey: Prentice Hall.

George, B. (2007) *True north: discover your authentic leadership.* New York: John Wiley & Sons.

Hunt, A. and Thomas, D. (1999) *The pragmatic programmer.* Reading, MA: Addison Wesley.

Larman, C. (2003) *Agile and iterative development: a manager's guide.* Boston, MA: Addison-Wesley.

Leffingwell, D. (2011) *Agile software requirements. Lean requirements practices for teams, programmes and the enterprise.* Upper Saddle River, NJ: Addison-Wesley.

Leffingwell, Dean (2007) *Scaling software agility: best practices for large organisations.* Upper Saddle River, NJ: Addison-Wesley.

Martin, Robert C. (2011) *The clean coder – a code of conduct for professional programmers.* New Jersey: Prentice Hall.

Martin, Robert C. (2009) *Clean code: a handbook of Agile software craftsmanship*. New Jersey: Prentice Hall.

Palmer, Stephen R. and Felsing, John M. (2002) *A practical guide to feature driven development*. New Jersey: Prentice Hall.

Peters, Prof Steve (2012) *The chimp paradox: the mind management programme to help you achieve success, confidence and happiness*. London: Vermilion.

Poppendieck, Mary and Poppendieck, Tom (2009) *Leading Lean software development: results are not the point*. Upper Saddle River, NJ: Addison-Wesley.

Reinertsen, Donald (1997) *Managing the design factory: a product developer's toolkit*. New York: The Free Press.

Robinson, Alan G. and Schroeder, D. M. (2014) *The idea-driven organisation: unlocking the power in bottom-up ideas*. San Francisco, CA: Berrett-Koehler.

Senge, Peter M. (2006) *The fifth discipline: the art and practice of the learning organisation*. London: Random House.

Shalloway, A., Beaver, G. and Trott, J. (2010) *Lean–Agile software development: achieving enterprise agility*. Upper Saddle River, NJ: Addison-Wesley.

Smith, Preston and Reinertsen, Donald (1998) *Developing products in half the time*. New York: John Wiley & Sons.

Sutherland, J. and Altman, I. (2010) 'Organisational transformation with Scrum: how a venture capital group gets twice as much done with half the work'. *System Sciences*, 1–9.

Wynne, Matt and Hellesoy, Aslak (2012) *The cucumber book: behaviour driven development for testers and developers*. Dallas, TX: Pragmatic Bookshelf.

INDEX